ME... ...FUD
W... Coincidence

Terry Duff

(Wee Glasgow Guy)

Grosvenor House
Publishing Limited

All rights reserved
Copyright © Terry Duff, 2024

The right of Terry Duff to be identified as the author of this
work has been asserted in accordance with Section 78
of the Copyright, Designs and Patents Act 1988

The book cover is copyright to Terry Duff

This book is published by
Grosvenor House Publishing Ltd
Link House
140 The Broadway, Tolworth, Surrey, KT6 7HT.
www.grosvenorhousepublishing.co.uk

This book is sold subject to the conditions that it shall not, by way of
trade or otherwise, be lent, resold, hired out or otherwise circulated
without the author's or publisher's prior consent in any form of
binding or cover other than that in which it is published and
without a similar condition including this condition being
imposed on the subsequent purchaser.

A CIP record for this book
is available from the British Library

Paperback ISBN 978-1-83615-066-4
eBook ISBN 978-1-83615-067-1

Dedication

I dedicate this book to Cheryl, Mirren, Mason and the Gorman family for their continued support.

To
The people of Whiteinch

Terry

Acknowledgement

I would like to thank my parents for the gift of life, like to thank the gift of life for me having so much fun. Thank fun for giving me a wonderful life. Thank wonderful life for the opportunity to write this book. Thank this book for giving other people the chance to enjoy my life. I would also like to thank all my family and friends with special mention to Susanne who proof read and helped to find the spelling and grammar mistakes.

Meet yrret ffud what a coincidence.

A quick explanation about the title, I moved to Australia when I was 40 years of age as a transfer for work. When I got there, I tried to set up an email, however there was a marketing guru in New Zealand called Terry Duff who had all the email addresses stitched up, so I decided to go backwards and that is the meet yrret ffud. The part named what a coincidence is because of all the strange coincidences that have happened throughout my life.

I was born on the 4th of December 1958 at 49 Northinch Street Whiteinch Glasgow which was strange in itself as the family home was no 55 which was previously my Auntie Margaret's house. 49 Northinch Street was where the sweet shop was and there was a little flat at the rear where my bed was the bottom drawer in the chest of drawers in the corner. My two brothers aged three and five were playing hide the light at 55 (paper set on fire) and one of them couldn't find it, the fire brigade did though and so we were all decanted out to various homes hence the sweetshop.

Father Robert who worked as a stager (Scaffolder nowadays) in the shipyards and mum worked in various cleaning jobs including Hamilton Crescent School, Claude Alexander the tailors and Greaves Sports all in Partick.

I was the youngest of the six brothers, Robert, Adam (Kenny), Alexander (My Hero), James, John. Mum always wanted a girl and sure that is why she kept trying, allegedly there is a photograph somewhere in the family where I am sitting on the sideboard dressed as a girl!!!

We moved from Whiteinch in 1960 because of the Clyde Tunnel being built and moved to the housing scheme of Knightswood, the biggest in Glasgow at the time.

We always had music around the house and had the old gramophone with 78rpm records and when I was three I could go through all the records and pick out one which was My Old Man's a Dustman by Glasgow singer songwriter Lonnie Donegan, lots of the records came from the same labels and had the same colours so it was no mean feat, my first introduction to what would be a fairly musical life.

My childhood was brilliant as we had the University playing fields at the back of us and a large piece of spare ground which the Garscadden Burn runs through. Jumping the burn was a great pastime and you gradually build up courage to take on the Geronimo, the large jump where the burn turned. On the spare ground we played football, rugby, cricket, golf and many more sports. We used to get nets and cricket paraphernalia from Mr Gabitas who was the caretaker of the University fields. We also lived not far from Knightswood Golf Course and from the age of five after school I would dash home grab my clubs and head there for nine holes or just practice at the 4th hole, which was a short par three, I would be there until dark, or someone came to get me. When I went to Australia, I told all my new mates there that I played at Royal Knightswood, one year when I was home, I took a couple of photographs and really disappointed them.

I went to Garscadden Primary school 100 yards from my home. John and James took me on my first day going in through the gates at Hurlford Avenue. I was only in until lunchtime and thought a great idea would be to make my own way home, unfortunately I came out the gates at Dunwan Avenue and proceeded to get lost, I was found quickly but I think that was my first desire to travel of which I have roughly flown 2,000,000 miles to date. I loved primary school and don't think I missed many days there. The other thing I remember was Carol Ann and her white socks, I had never seen socks that colour before, she was an only girl and did not get the hand me downs like most of the other kids. I loved Garscadden School, my brothers went there, my daughter Cheryl went there, and my granddaughter Mirren went there too. But sadly, they knocked it down and it is now houses.

We also played football out in the street at night with the gates being the goals, not too many cars to worry about at that time but there was the occasional close shave with a vehicle or a bicycle. This was a great grounding for all the potential footballers in the area as you normally played with a tennis ball, my brother Alexander who suffered all his life with Muscular Dystrophy was great at this game, and his close control was a joy to behold.

I played football for the school team and also the Boys Brigade teams of 198 and 270 where I was quite successful and scored many goals, I could play all over the park from goalkeeper through to left winger and

I was a rare talent at that time as I could play well with both feet, well I kind of needed both feet to do it!

I left primary school in July 1969 enjoyed summer holidays and then went to the big school which was Victoria Drive in Scotstoun where I was in the top class 1R, after the morning assembly we were asked to vote a class captain which was strange as we hardly knew each other but lo and behold the Duffster won that one, yes that was my nickname. My last class in the morning was Maths and I met my new teacher Mr Kushal, he asked who the class captain was, and he asked my name and when I said Terry Duff, he said Duff oh no not another one obviously having met some of my brothers.

I sat beside my good friend Steven Donald in some classes, and we had so much fun making all sorts of trouble in class, which probably explains why I came 31st out of 33 in the class halfway through term and he was 31st and I was 33rd at end of term, now demotion down to 1D. The classes were named after the word Camperdown, girls were C to E and boys R to N I didn't have too far to travel to get to the bottom but stayed in the d for the next few years. I did not like secondary school, not sure why but just couldn't take it at all. This led me to take time away from the place not officially though, my good friend Matthew BUD Abbott and I found all sorts of places to go during school hours. John Cameron's house was a good one as his parents were out all day at work, the Kelvingrove Art Galleries when it was raining and around the golf courses and parks when it was dry.

My brother John dogged it (different meaning nowadays) for 18 months and he only got caught because he and James had a falling out and James grassed him up. The school board came to the house and lo and behold it was my Auntie Betty Heron, she took him back and introduced him to Mr Bell the English teacher who couldn't remember who he was. Bud and I didn't get secondary school and spent a lot of time touring the city of Glasgow. While doing these tours and travels of the city we were in the Central Train Station one day when a large crowd gathered, and we had to see what was happening. We got to the front, and it was Jeremy Thorpe the MP being interviewed right in front of us and it led to us being in full view on the six o'clock news. I had a bit of explaining to do there but think I got away with it. Not so the next one though, the school had a wooden annexe and one day when I came home from school Mum asked me what all the commotion was at the school today, I said it was just a training exercise, once again the six o'clock news caught me out as the Annexe had burnt to the ground and I received a few slaps for that one.

I used to stay at Stevie's now and again in 64 Fulwood Avenue and sleep in the backroom, it was just around the corner from my house, but it was good to get away and get a different meal from Mrs Donald. Watch out for this one later.

I played football for a very good team called Drumchapel Amateurs who are very famous in the Glasgow area having produced such great players as Sir Alex Ferguson, Asa Hartford, Archie Gemmell, David Moyes, and John Wark who I also went to school with. David Moyes' dad was our coach. The club was founded by Englishman Douglas Smith, and he concentrated his efforts in helping the community get some relief from the dark days. The teams that we played against all come from areas where poverty was rife, Eastercraigs (Easterhouse), Possil YM, Harmony Row (Govan) Pollok United and a few more. The club used to send a letter on a Wednesday to tell you who you were playing and where and when to meet. We had blazers white shirt and tie and a Drumchapel Amateurs bag for the kit and a compartment for dirty boots. The faces on the opposing teams were a picture and I am sure they gave us a two goal start most games. The club played in many European tournaments playing teams like Real Madrid, Inter Milan, and many more famous teams. I played in one tournament that was unfortunately at Shieldhall in Glasgow, not the sunny climates of Spain or Italy. I remember we played Manchester United but did not know any of their players but sure some went on to fame. It was around this time that I am sure I played against Mr Talksport Alan Brazil before he went on to become a great player initially alongside John Wark at Ipswich. Also in my class at school was a guy called George Watt who went on to form the group Big George and the Business and he wrote music for TV and the movies as well as being a fantastic guitarist with a gruff voice, his bandmate Tam McLucas also went to our school.

I went down to Leeds United on a trial and was doing okay, it was the Don Revie days and there were so many great players at the time especially Scotsmen Billy Bremner, Peter Lorimer, Eddie Gray, even the reserves were stacked with David Harvey, Gordon McQueen, and Joe Jordan. It was a short stint, and I can now reveal the real reason I left, and hitch hiked back to Glasgow. I peed the bed, not every night but a few times and it really embarrassed me, my hosts were great about it, but I felt I couldn't take it anymore. I hitch hiked it from Leeds, I got home at 4.00am in the morning and my family were all going crazy, police had been out all over the place looking for me and I am sure many slaps were due, however my life was saved when oldest brother Robert came in and told mum that she was going to be a granny PHEW, I was quickly forgotten about, thank you nephew James.

I also played cricket at school and was captain of the team, it was great as you got an afternoon off to play and I loved it. I have not been to the cricket in the UK but did go to the boxing-day test between Australia and

South Africa at the Sydney Cricket Ground and saw the West Indies at the Gabba in Brisbane when Chris Gayle a giant of a man smashed the Australian bowlers all over the place.

I loved music and had watched Stealers Wheel with stuck in the middle with you on Top of the Pops and then went out to play football in the street. As I was running out on the road a guy passed me on a bike and I shouted that was the guy that was just on Top of the Pop's, and I got the usual don't talk rubbish comments.

I had started my second job around this time as a milk boy in the Clydebank area, a suburb not far from home. I loved the early mornings even in the winter. One Friday I was collecting the money and lo and behold who comes to the door but no other than Gerry Rafferty of Stealers Wheel, I was gobsmacked but immediately knew I was right that night. This job took its toll on my education!!! Getting up so early in the morning meant when I got into a nice warm classroom, I would fall asleep. One of the classes we had a visit from a brain specialist called Dr Bahkshish from Hungary, he had with him a brain in a jar and seemingly the brain and I were very closely related when I fell asleep at the front of the class. I was tapped on the shoulder and wakened to the jar right beside me, sorry Doctor.

On a summer camping trip to Southend south of Campbelltown we went into the local hotel, not old enough to drink but it had a pool table. We were playing a few games when some guys came in, scruffy looking with long hair, they came over and put their names on the board and as soon as I saw the first initials I clicked. DL were the initials, and I told the guys that it was Denny Laine from Wings and previously of the Moody Blues, I approached him and he told us he was in the area writing some songs which I take it they were staying probably on Paul McCartney's farm which was in the area.

We used to spend a lot of time at the Knightswood Community Centre, which was great, I was quite good at Table Tennis and played for the club in the league. We also played basketball and had great record nights as well. A couple of the guy's Kevin and Glen were into the Heavy Metal genre like Kiss, but it was great for everybody to have their say on what was played, it opened my eyes up to different styles of music. This was where Bud and I performed our first disco using borrowed decks and records, it went down a treat and we got requested to do more, thinking back we should have charged for them. One night Les one of the older leaders brought in a record, he was a rep for record companies and so began the life of our new name "Sanfrandisco" the record was Sanfrancisco by the Village People. This is also where Bud met his good lady Margaret, and they are still together to this day. We started hanging around with Jim McDonald also our age and one of the boys, we met loads of new people at that time.

We also had a couple of great outings to Blairvadach Outdoor Facility back then too. Gordon MacKenzie was the organiser from the Community Centre. First time I went we were canoeing, and we did some local stuff on the water at Rhu which gave us the confidence to go and canoe around Loch Lomond which was great, we ended up doing barrel rolls and it was very exhilarating when you came up from the cold water. I actually went canoeing with another club a few years later at Strathclyde Country Park and we are asked to do rolls and I was in shallow water and got stuck in the mud, I panicked and managed to get out before anyone got to me but it took most of the skin off my leg getting out, no more for me.

The next trip we went to climb the Cobbler peak in Arrochar, and half of the group got off in Arrochar, that was our group and half went around the other side of the peak. The idea was that we would meet at the top, have lunch and we would go down the opposite side we had climbed. We were given packed lunches and as we were going up a lot of us were looking at the packed lunch, sandwiches, water, apple, oat cake. What on earth is an oat cake, this was promptly dumped in the first bin. The snow was up to our knees and the guide we had was his first time on the Cobbler. We got three quarters of the way up and the mist was coming down and he suggested we stop. He pulled out a big sheet, threw it up in the air and we all grabbed it and put it under our bums to create a tent of sorts. It is at this time that he has the compass out and suggests we shouldn't eat all our packed lunch just in case, what do you mean just in case. We ended up coming back down the same way following our footsteps and walking around the road to get the van to pick up the rest of the group up who completed the challenge.

Canoe Gang,
Hillwalkers and
Jim and I in the Hostel

After watching Top of the Pops on Thursday the 4th of November 1974, I went out to the street to play football, my dad had been complaining of not being well and soon an Ambulance turned up, as he was being carried out, I told him I would come and see him tomorrow. At 5.00am on the 5th November my brother Kenny woke me and told me dad had passed away, I was 15 at the time. Coincidently the 5th of November 1939 was when his dad had died also. My dad and two of his brothers went to war and successfully survived but on the 8th of November Alexander died and on the 22nd John passed away. Three young men survived a war, and all died within 17 days of each other. Still on the subject of the 5th of November 1979 my gran died, my dad's mum, hence when the 5th comes around I try not to do too much. One of my ex-employers once told me to stay at home, don't do anything today but stay in bed and pull the blankets over my head. NO don't pull the blankets over your head. In the middle of the year 1975 on the 29th June just months after dad had passed mum was taken from us. Funny mum and dad never really argued that I remember, only times she was angry with him was when he would be drunk. My dad and his mate Big Alan Dunn from along the street used to go to the pub on a Saturday and when they were coming back, they would stop at the corner just before Alan's house and sit and sing at the top of their voices, both good singers right enough. This was a good 50 yards from our house, but mum was always sitting at the window smoking, and she would say to whoever was available, right go and get him. Another time he fell in the burn taking a shortcut home when he got in, he was soaking wet and started to strip, mum turned to him to tell him to go into the room but unfortunately, she forgot she had the teapot in her hand and skelped him right on the nose with the spout splitting his nose open, all he could do was laugh. Mum was a heavy smoker, sometimes 60 a day, dad and four brothers smoked as well. When Celtic won the European Cup in 1967, I had to watch it lying on the floor to see underneath the smoke cloud. When mum passed away, she did so with 2 fingers at her mouth as if she had a cigarette in her hand.

Dad, Alex and John, David, John, Alex, Dad, Daniel, Babs, Margaret, Gran, Cissy and Cathy and Dad in the desert, says Hitler's nightmare Bonnie Scotland on the board

On a trip to Knightswood Park with my then girlfriend we were following a girl with a pram and a youngster running around the pond area. After a few minutes I noticed the wee fella had disappeared and

I ran ahead and there he was rolling around in the pond with the mother not even knowing what had happened. I pulled him out and got him on the grass, turns out he was fine but not sure how much longer he could have survived as the water was very cold. No thanks were received.

I left school in December 1974 and looked for a job, Bud and I had seen an advert which was a printing and bookbinding company HB Langman in York Street Glasgow looking for two messengers. Bud had a long leather coat, and I had a denim jacket and we decided to toss to see who went in first and then to see who wore the coat, he won both. He came out with the job. When I went in the lady who was interviewing said that the last person who was in came from the same school and did, I know him, I said I had heard of him but didn't know him too well, I got the job too.

We started on the 11th of January 1975 and our roles were to basically go to the shops for 60 women and 20 men, there was a Henry Healy's at the corner of York Street and Argyle Street, and we were sent there for the lunches, we also got sent to hardware stores and other shops for various other things, they sent us to the bank with thousands of pounds to bank. It was an okay job but again we got up to mischief like dropping the paperweights on top of the old fashion lift to frighten the operator Kenny, one time Bud put too big a weight through the bars, and it went straight through the lift top and bottom just missing Kenny. We were paid £10.50 a week, and everybody got paid on the Friday before lunch except us two in case we didn't come back, as mentioned we were sent to the bank with thousands and if we weren't coming back, it wouldn't have been for the wages. One Friday after a few months we went down to get the wages, the lady gave Bud his wages and his P45 (Leaving document) and she handed me my wages, I asked where is my P45 she said I did not have one and that they were thinking of giving me an apprenticeship, I replied if he has his P45 I want my P45 and fifteen minutes later we left HB Langman for the last time.

Next stop was the Clydebank Co-op looking for a storeman, we both went in to do an initial casual interview and again tossed for the coat and who went in first. I won both and Bud told me that the office was up to the right and as I went that way, he shot up the stairs and into the recruitment office, luckily, he failed, and I got the job. The store was in Cochno Street Clydebank, it used to service all the shops in the area with stock. The order sheets were processed by a couple of older guys, and I noticed very quickly that in some cases it would ask for a block of cheese and three or four were loaded onto the delivery truck for personal sale to other shops and family. I used to go home for lunch and cut through the lane at the side of the building, I looked up and saw there were air vents there and started thinking.

When I went back to work, I went upstairs and pulled away large cereal boxes and saw the vents from the inside. One day before leaving I kicked the vents in and then went round and found them in the lane, plan started. When going home for lunch I would take a 6lb tin of gammon, corned beef, or chopped pork, drop it in the lane and then get it and sell it to the McDonald family along the street. One night while out with a couple of friends I hatched the big one, I stacked up a load of tins behind the cereal boxes and Tony and Norrie were in the lane to gather them and get them away. Unfortunately, there was a woman washing her dishes on the other side of the lane who witnessed all these flying tins of meat and reported it to the police. In the afternoon they came and interviewed me, and I denied all knowledge however I decided to quit the job as I could not handle the suspicion from fellow colleagues!!!

I had passed the test at school to go to Yarrows the shipbuilders and had two trips there to see it, did not like the look of it one little bit and decided it was not for me. I did manage to get an apprenticeship as a TV Engineer with Clyde Factors based at Finnieston in Glasgow right opposite the Finnieston Crane which still sits there to this day. I worked alongside another five apprentices and two time served engineers. I learned a good bit and was doing quite well but discovered a nice loophole in that we had an outside toilet and the postman came around 9.30am and if you had not attended college on your day release we would all take turns of going to the toilet to collect the mail, whip out the Cardonald College letters and pass the rest to the administration girl. I learned that from the other apprentices, one of whom got me into being a pub DJ.

Bert worked at a pub called the Three Pigeons in Charing Cross which was famous for its function suites and organised parties for everything from 21st birthdays to weddings. I got £15 a week for my apprenticeship and £15 a night for being a DJ, no brainer not recognising at the time the importance of a good steady career. I quit the apprenticeship in 2nd year and worked six nights a week in the Three Doo's as it was commonly known. I had some great nights there. One night in the downstairs function suite we had an all women party and there were around 60 there ranging in age from I would say 16 to 80. I made a little joke just after the start of the night and I said I was getting the latest news in my ear through the headphones, and I went on the microphone and gave out the news. It has just been confirmed that Louis Armstrong was still dead, one of the older women approached me and I thought she was going to ask for a request instead she slapped me, and everyone was in hysterics including me. It actually was a great night and midway through it I started a conga in the middle of the dance floor and everybody joined in but it was a bit crowded so up the stairs we went out on to Granville Street turn right into Sauchiehall Street turn right into North Street turn right on to Berkeley Street and turn right again back to Granville Street then back down the stairs and finished in the middle of the dance floor all clapping each other.

Another night there was on Engagement party downstairs when it was invaded by Bayern Munich and St Étienne football fans who were in Glasgow for the European Cup Final at Hampden, they had seemingly heard the music and about 30 of them turned up. I approached the couple and told them we would get them out and they said don't bother as they are all enjoying themselves and everyone did for the rest of the night. I got many cuddles that night not from the Glaswegians but the team's fans.

Brothers Alexander and James played guitar and John fancied himself as David Bowie and I had a set of drums, so we formed a kind of family band, but Alexander left as he was getting well into his darts career by then and John moved to London. So, James and I found another couple of guys, and we performed a couple of gigs. I had bought the drums from a shop in Whiteinch for £65 and practiced in the house in Alderman Road driving the neighbour's nuts even though I had towels over the skins. We were decanted to High Knightswood for a while so they could modernise the building and change the flat roof (Stupid idea for a country that has so much rain) to peak roofs. One night

I decided to have a practice on the drums before going to the Three Doo's and as soon as I started the walls were banging and I stopped immediately not knowing who our new neighbours were. Next night I was sitting in my bedroom when I heard next door's budgie chirping away, what did the drums sound like to them and the budgie, I do apologise to all. I then took the drums back to the shop in Whiteinch and sold them back to the guy for £90 and I believe that was the start of my sales career. I went to visit John in London and arrived on the Saturday mid-morning, he opened the door and his face was all cut and scratched and when I asked what happened he told me he had been mugged again, turns out this was the fourth time. I asked if he had reported it to the police and he said no and when I questioned why he says what do I tell them, a group of guys dark in colour all wearing black leather jackets, white t-shirts, denims and white trainers seemingly all the young ones in the area wear the same clothes so that they cannot be identified if committing crime. I suggested we go for a beer and he said we could walk to the Mitre Bar and I said no way as he had just been mugged for the fourth time. We walked up to a metal hatch which John told me was where you ordered your taxis. He chapped it and a huge guy opens it and asks where we are going, slams it shut and a minute or so later our taxi turns up. It is an old Datsun Cherry with no radio for fares and in fact no radio just wires hanging out. I get in the front and John gets in the back and in real broken English the guy asks us how we get there, John directs him through the back streets to the Mitre Bar, he then asks how much and I say two quid while John says a fiver, we give him the fiver and he asks how to get back and I suggest to John let me guide him back, I reckon he could still be driving around London to this day!!!

James and John both played for a local football team called Hillhead Baptist which was supposed to be a church team, but no one had been near the church. The team was run by a lovely man called Neil MacKinnon, the team was made up of three McCormack's, three Gow's, three McKee's and two Duffs. All very good players and the team was quite successful winning league and cups for a few years until some of the team lost interest and started to break up. Susanne my good lady worked with a lady called Jean who was deaf and dumb and many years later we were invited to her house and sitting in his chair was Neilly who was by now very old. Jean went to introduce me, and I said no need as I know your father and proceeded to make an old man very happy reminiscing about his football team. We went to Jeans wedding and then on to the disco at the Deaf and Dumb club in Glasgow, yes this is true, the floor vibrates, and people can judge how to dance but believe it or not it was extremely loud as they all shout at each other. I had seen this before playing a football match at the fifty pitches where both teams on the pitch next to us were deaf and dumb but it was very noisy as they tried to express themselves verbally.

I had quit the Three Doo's by then and moved to London for a change, I stayed with Kenny, Helen and kids Robert and Tara in Kentish Town, he had moved there many years before. I got a job in Oxford Street as a storeman in Baber's, a high-class shoe store where I used to send shoes all over the world and a lot to Australia which was a country which intrigued me. I used to deliver shoes to the Australian Embassy as well. I also used to send shoes to my brother Kenny to assist in paying for my staying in his house. One night I went to see the group Tavares perform at the Old Vic Theatre with Heatwave being the support act. It was a great night and still to this day Bud's wife Margaret calls me Terry Tavares. I used to go to the same pub every night to give Kenny, Helen and the kids some time together and every night the barman asked me what I wanted, for 7 months he asked me and I had the same drink every night. I was in one Saturday and Liverpool and Manchester United had played the cup final of 1977, all the fans were mingling together and getting on well, the place was mobbed, and the barman was delighted. I got talking to a big group of fans and told them there was a great pub just along the road, great music, and lovely ladies. Ten minutes later I walked out of the pub with around sixty fans and went to the pub down the road making sure I looked at the barman on the way out. Goodbye Bull and Gate.

I came back from London and went back to Alderman Road where only Alexander and James remained, Alexander had his girlfriend staying with him and every now and then there would be a flare up between us all, James and I decided to move out and in fact James moved to London to stay and work with Kenny. I had a very lucky escape one night and it just reiterates the saying about not cooking with a drink in you. I was making chips in the old fashioned way with oil and went to take the basket out of the pan and didn't lift it high enough and toppled the pan, I managed to jump away but lot of burning fat went over my jeans and I managed to get them off before it got through to my skin. I have never since or will again cook when I am drinking unless it is a BBQ outside.

I got a job marking the board in the bookies way before televisions were put into the shops. It was commentary only via the Tannoy. The shop was at the corner of Dumbarton Road and Burnham Road near to where Yarrows the shipbuilders was. They had 4000 employees at that time and loads of them would come into the shop to place their bets, but many also came in to eat their lunch especially when it was raining. Others used to head for the two pubs that were there, The Dry Dock and The Smugglers Inn to consume their lunchtime pints and whiskeys before running back to work. A pub further away, The Station Bar organised buses to pick them up and drop them off again and the bar was loaded with pre poured drinks for speed. Back to the Bookies and one guy I had so much fun with and created great fun for many more people. This guy was always first in and last out at lunchtime then first in again after finishing work where he would scour the boards for his results. He used to put on many bets with seven and eight horses and dogs and my boss Vince hated it as it took a long time to settle them. When he checked his results, he would come to me and ask how they had all got on. My favourite response one day had the whole shop in stitches apart from him. He had a few up and his last one was second and he wanted the story. Right here we go, It was in the lead and jumped the last fence well clear but the jockey came off, he held on to the horse and ran beside it before managing to get back on only for the saddle to slip and he was thrown off the other side of the horse, he kept the reins and managed to get back on the bareback of the horse only for him to get pipped on the line. Great work by the jockey but not so good for him, he was gutted however the rest of the punters in the shop were in hysterics but in reality, it was well beaten. One of the punters an old fella called Hector MacDonald called me over and commented how I was always smiling and laughing, then he whispered to me, son are you on that MariJuana and that is exactly how he said it, I assured him I was not and never would be.

TERRY DUFF (WEE GLASGOW GUY)

I moved from marking the board to another company where I became settler manager in a small shop in Scotstoun. It was the time when there were no duplicate betting slips and you wrote your horses on a piece of paper or postcard with a nom de plume as your identifier, you got a slip from the till which your nom de plume was written on.

There was an elderly lady called Annie who used to come in with her bets, she walked on the side of her feet and wobbled as she walked. She handed me her bets and I swear to God I could not make out anything that she had written except she still had old money as the value to pay. I tried very hard but struggled, when she came in the next day, I gave her a pound and said she had a good day. Every day I gave Annie money, some days it was a pound and some occasional days when the shop had a good day, I would give her ten pounds. She told me that since I started in the shop that I had brought great luck to her betting. One day Annie didn't turn up and sadly she had passed hopefully a rich woman!!!

Another punter used to bet on the Snooker and the Darts when the World Championships were on. He used to come in with his beautiful daughter and his nom de plume was Cheryl, and she had the most beautiful smile and laugh when I used to shout her name, more to follow on this.

I moved to another shop in Partick where Billy Connolly's dad used to come into, one day he came to collect his bet and I had to tell him that he was late putting his bet on and I couldn't pay him the full amount, he took what I gave him and never came back. Turns out the internal clock on the till was wrong, sorry Billy's dad. I had a run in with the boss about it and he didn't seem that bothered so I left.

I was unemployed again and along with a few other mates we used to get our benefits on different days and we would go to Knightswood Golf Course and whoever had the money would jump the burn at the 5th hole, get their money and get the carry out for the day. It was a beautiful summer, and we would sit there on the tee sometimes for up to six hours letting everyone go past, when we were ready, we would generally just walk off without finishing. Seemingly the guy in the clubhouse would ask people who had just finished if we were still out there. We would then head back to the local pub The Forum to finish the day off. In 1984 we played golf at Dougalston Golf Course and spent the afternoon watching Seve Ballesteros win the British Open in the company of one Derek Johnstone the former Rangers player. It was a great afternoon even though I had fallen in the sewage swamp trying to retrieve my ball, metal golf spikes on round metal pipes don't go well together, luckily they had showers and I had a change of clothes.

One day George Benson and I, not the singer but a mate, went to the Lovat Arms, a pub just on the boundary with Yoker and Clydebank. We were going up the road and a girl called Caroline joined us for the short walk, she had brought her drink with her from the pub. After about 50 yards at the lane leading to Yoker Bowling Club she said she needed to pee, she went down the lane which is an upside down L shape, she was away ages and I suggested to George he go and get her, he went down the lane and started shouting on me, as I got there she was trying to slash her wrists, I grabbed her and she swung her hands and cut me under the chin. I was bleeding heavily, and I have to admit that I did lash out at her to try and drag her away, however the next thing was lights going on and dogs barking, and doors being opened. George and I ran to his house where his mum gave me towels to try and stop the bleeding and gave me a change of shirt. We were there five minutes when the police cars arrived, and we were taken to Partick Marine Police Station for questioning. They obviously interviewed her first and we were there for many hours, we were basically being accused of attempted rape and they kept saying things like you're going down for this which frightened the crap out of me and seemingly George as well. In the questioning the officer said that you tried to smash the glass that she had her drink in into her face and that she had bruising on her face. I did tell him that I had lost the plot a bit, but I was only trying to stop her harming herself and then I said wait a minute did you say glass, yes, I said it was a beer bottle not a glass. They then sent someone down the lane and retrieved the bottle and in the meantime, they had background checks and found she had a history of it, released without charge. This was in the early 1980's and I never saw the woman again, however in 2014 we were away for the weekend on Bud's boat in Loch Lomond and when we came back we went to Yoker Bowling Club for a few beers, we left to go to the Station Bar across the road and there was a van parked in the lane and as the four of us went one way four women were coming around the other side of the van, Bud asked me if I knew who that was and I said no, he said Caroline and I nearly fainted I swear as this was literally five yards from where the incident happened.

Big Mick who ran the Forum pub used to run a bus down for the Grand National weekend, we would leave Friday morning and arrive in the afternoon at Southport Pontin's Holiday Camp and stay Friday Saturday and Sunday nights and back Monday. To be honest most people never went to the races just watched it on TV, but they were great laughs all weekend. We did go one year in 1981 to the famous Aintree Racecourse. It cost seven pounds on a coach leaving from the camp, one pound for the bus and six for the entry into the racing. Tony, Davie, Norrie, and I were all geared up, we each had our carry outs ready for the big day. We arrived early at the track and at the time you could go on the track and look at the hurdles and fences. We stood at the last hurdle, how can a horse fall at that? We then stood at the chair and what a monster of a fence that was. We were in the furthest away area of the track you could get but when we heard the helicopter coming in to land and all the crowd facing the other way, we were no longer in the cheap seats. Over the fence and into the crowd we were in the main stand now right near the finishing line and just in from the parade ring. We went down to the bookies area, and I suggested we get our bets on early so the boys bet Rathgorman and I bet Badsworth Boy at 7/2 for five pounds, twenty-two pounds fifty back when he wins. Both horses were trained by Michael Dickinson and when we walked to the parade ring who were we standing beside but none other than the great man. We then walked around and the boys in front started going up a staircase. Next minute two policemen caught us, we were only trying to get into the Press Box but there was a guy standing in front of the sign, so we never saw it. Can we see your passes, nope, can we see your tickets, nope, okay out you go and they promptly threw us out. We had to pay another six pounds to get in and the first race was just about to go. Tony's (Tony's as blind as a bat) got the binoculars out to see the six runners, how are they going Tony they were over the far side, yep all going well just as he said it we heard the hoofs pounding towards our position and it was number 1 Rathgorman, it had unseated his rider not long after the start, so Tony not all going well. Coming to the last and Badsworth Boy is 20 lengths clear so I start my rant, not cheering a winner on but fall you bastard, fall you bastard, fall you bastard and luckily enough he did kicking the jockey as he went down and the boys are screaming at me what you doing you lunatic, you had a winner and you wanted it to fall, you are nuts, no I'm not I calmly said, I put it on in there pointing to the main stand and it would cost me twenty quid to get in to collect it and we had already paid back in here so twenty six quid outlay to collect twenty two fifty, don't think so, who is nuts now. Apologies to Robert Earnshaw the jockey for getting you a sore one. Not a good day, I had two falls at the last, two fell at the first, a second and a second last. One of the falls at the last would have been a winner but it fell at that last tiny hurdle that I had suggested no horse should fall at. Also, big thank you to Charles and Diana for allowing us to at least see the parade ring at Aintree, that was who came in on the helicopter. When we got back to the camp, I had a few and then went to bed early I mean around 10.00pm. Next morning, I hear lots of movement and people packing their bags, what is happening here I asked? Well, last night security had a go at us for being too rowdy and Billy took the guys hat off and poured a pint over him, he said that had never happened to him once in all his years there, so Billy done it again hence we

TERRY DUFF (WEE GLASGOW GUY)

were all thrown out of Pontin's Holiday Camp in Southport.

On my last trip to Southport we went to Anfield on the Saturday morning for the Liverpool v Sheffield Wednesday game which was played early because of the Grand National. We were in the Kop end and commenting on the fences that were used in England but not Scotland. The crowd around us warned us that when Liverpool scored we were just to go with the sway forward and then back. I have asthma and a bit claustrophobic and when Liverpool scored their fourth I told the guys I had to leave, we all left and the game finished 5-1. The following Saturday we were at Parkhead for the Scottish Cup semi-final with St Johnstone and there was a crush and the wall way down in front of us collapsed and some people went on the pitch to escape, this was around the exact same time when the Hillsborough disaster took place. One of the guys near us had a radio and he said reports were coming in about fighting taking place at Hillsborough and fans on the pitch, it didn't take long for that message to be completely changed.

I was getting a bit too heavy into the drink and decided to see the doctor to advise him that I was becoming an alcoholic and wanted to do something about it. He asked if I was very sure, and he prescribed Antabuse tablets that would make me violently ill if I took alcohol with them. This is the same stuff that was seemingly sown into George Best's stomach. I started them on Monday and took them until Thursday, the weekend was coming. I went out Friday with my brother James and mate Spindoe to the Elderslie pub in Yoker to play pool, when I went to the bar the manager Harry asked if I was okay and I said yes, he told me to look in the mirror and my face was covered in red blotches. Didn't know what it was and put it down to the heat in the place, we left there and went to the Forum where I had one pint of cider and told the boys I had to go home where I was violently ill as prescribed. I decided at that time that I would need to give up, so I stopped taking the tablets. It really is a great way to assist with alcoholism, but I just wasn't ready as all my activities at the time involved pubs, DJ, playing pool and out with my mates.

I was captain of the Forum pool team, and we had a great year which culminated in me winning Clydebank and District player of the year, the following year I was joint winner. We had some great times with the pool team as we were all characters and had great fun.

Bud Jim and I used to go into the town on a Friday night to the Tyrol Bar at Anderston and go for a few beers before heading back to the Forum for the disco that was on. One night when we went back, I met Gina. She was from Queenslie and used to come through and stay with her sister Isabel in Yoker, we got chatting and ended up going out together. We moved in together and we moved around a bit staying at various addresses around the area.

My mates used to take time off for Cheltenham races and we would have a couple of days together betting and a few beers. On the Thursday I had two pounds left and was going to do a one-pound double on the races that were not on TV in the pub. In walks the gypsy woman with the little pup and yup I bought it for a pound as the little thing was shivering and scratching away. I decided to get a taxi up the road with my other pound and as we were sitting at the roundabout a commotion was taking place at the bus stop. A guy who I went to school with, his father had just got off the bus a bit the worse for wear, the schoolkids on the bus were taking the mickey out of him. Unfortunately, he slipped, and the back wheel of the bus ran over his head killing him instantly. Next day I get the newspapers and find out Reldis 9/1 and Political Pop 15/2 had both won, goodbye eighty-five quid and hello Sheba. I used to take Gina's sisters dog Rocco out for walks and one day took him to the unemployment exchange where you signed on for your unemployment benefit, standing in the queue talking to people the place erupted in laughter. I turn around to see Rocco coming to the end of his works in the middle of the floor, one of the staff came out and told me to clean it up and I said it wasn't me that done it, more hilarity, it was your dog that done it, sorry not my dog, two people came out from behind counter and cleaned up the mess.

We eventually got a ground floor flat in Langholm Street Yoker, the street was notorious at the time for criminal activities and violence. Sheba moved in with us and soon had damaged her leg on the veranda, trip to vet to get the plaster cast and proverbial lampshade to stop her biting her bandage. She was a lunatic this dog, she used to be able to open the doors in the house by putting her paw on the handle and walking backwards. She also used to eat anything from shoes to bedding, one day I went to go in the backroom after hearing a very large sound and could not get in. I went around to the back window and there was Sheba eating the bedclothes having managed to knock down a full-size wardrobe, I had to break the window to get in. It got to the stage that we had to put her in the kitchen and tie all the doors together, one day I went to the shops and came back, and Sheba was in the kitchen eating the lid of the spray that was supposed to stop her from eating things. We did take Rocky in as well; he was from full bred German Shepherd Rocco a beautiful specimen of a dog. We kept both for a while but was getting too much so we found a home for Sheba, and she was well looked after. One day we were at Isobel's who stayed upstairs in a four in a block, Rocco used to stand up and watch the world go by and Rocky was getting there too. The couple we gave Sheba to walked by with her and Rocky decided he wanted a closer view and to say hello to his old pal. Over he went breaking a leg which was lucky as it should have been a lot worse, back to the vet. On a trip to the vet one morning on the bus, we sat up towards the back and with all the school children fussing over him Rocky promptly threw up very impressively I may add, turns out his stomach was where the turning shaft rotated.

On June the second 1982 we had a new mattress delivered and I asked the guys to throw it on the bed which they did with the label facing up the way, Golden Fleece was the name on the mattress and also the favourite for the Derby that afternoon and it promptly won at 3/1. I had my usual pound on for four pound return.

We started planning for a baby, the baby we had agreed would be called Gemma however when I first saw our beautiful daughter there was only one name for her and Cheryl was born on the 26th of July 1984. Cheryl has grown up to be a fantastic mother to our grandkids Mirren and Mason and has continued to work whilst doing this.

A year before Cheryl was born my oldest brother Robert passed away aged thirty five. He had went to give blood six months before and they told him the results showed some anomalies in his blood and took him into the hospital and gave him blood transfusions to rectify but unfortunately it had the opposite effect.

My conclusion is that he had donated blood and a contaminated needle was used and then the blood transfusions were at the time of the UK contaminated blood scandal. Robert was a moderate drinker at the weekend but his doctor said he died from Hepatitis B and Cirrhosis of the Liver but he would have had to drink a bottle of whisky a day for his liver to be like that. He played snooker when younger and then moved onto pool where he played a couple of times for Scotland. Robert and Anne had three beautiful kids and it is a real shame that he never got to see them grown up, we had a family get together not long ago and it was great to see the three of them there.

James, Craig, Me, Lee-Anne, Cheryl Mirren and Mason

Bud and Margaret got married and Jim was the best man, why? I was told that it was because they didn't know if I would be back from London when they arranged it, I still dig them both about it, in fact I tell them I wasn't even invited but they know I was there.

Jim immigrated to Canada not long after this and still lives there to this day. I was back on holiday from Australia one time and had Bud's car. I was driving up where Jim used to live in Killoch Drive when two guys stepped out in front of me and I nearly ran them over, bit of a common theme you will find, and it turns out it was Jim and his son over visiting the family. We never got a chance to catch up at that time but did so later in life.

Gina's brother Sammy got me a job with a building company called Lafferty a well know Glasgow institution where Jimmy Johnstone the old Celtic player worked as a driver. I started work as a labourer on the Monday and had already told Sammy that I didn't do heights and he told me not to worry, second day right in front of the bosses office we have to load roof tile strapping on to the roof and I had to climb the scaffolding, it was five levels high and I got to the fourth and froze and he had to pull me up by the dungarees and after that I was fine even coming down after a shift on the cranes bucket. One Sunday while doing overtime which consisted cleaning up the site, that took us an hour and we were paid for five hours Willie Weir and I were sitting on the scaffolding having a beer. Willie had been telling me that his daughter had been waiting on a house and she finally got one in a place called Hamiltonhill, he asked if I knew it and I told him my dad and the rest of the family grew up there. I asked him where in Hamiltonhill and he told me Appleby Street, I said number 41 and he said that's right and then I said top floor flat on the left and again spot on, that was my granny's old flat.

Gina had suggested we get married so that Cheryl didn't go to school out of wedlock, and I suggested she organise it and I would turn up. She chose the 18th of November 1988, yes November the month that all my family died, yes November. I think this was a sign that this was not going to work but decided to go through with it for Cheryl's sake.

Bud and I went for a game of snooker on the morning of the wedding, and he advised me that I was doing the wrong thing but maybe for the right reason re Cheryl. We got married in Clydebank Registry Office Bud wasn't my best man Donald McDonald was (revenge?) We had the function in Oliver's Drumchapel after that we went to the dancing and the next day, I went on the supporter's bus to Dundee to watch the football, what a honeymoon. One of our big arguments was about my need to bring Cheryl up in a better street and preferably a house with a garden like the one I had come from in Alderman Road, but Gina loved the street and wasn't for moving. This got me thinking where I will be in five years or ten years and as mentioned the pub was too handy too. I kept suggesting this and kept getting rebuffed. The arguments were getting more and more, and I decided that it was time for me to leave. A year or so after I left Gina got the opportunity to do a house swap as a woman wanted to be in Langholm Street near her family. The swap went through, and Gina and Cheryl moved into a house in Fulwood Avenue, not any house but my mate Stevie's old house where Cheryl slept in the same room that I used to sleep in, guess what it had a back and front garden!!

We had been together for nine years and after nine months of marriage I left and went to sleep on Alexander's floor in Whiteinch for a while before getting a flat in Anderston near the centre of Glasgow which was handy for the shops and the pub the Pot Black which was even nearer than the Forum was to Langholm Street.

I did get a job; well, it was an employment scheme where you worked on a project and got an extra £10 a week for your wages. It was called Keep Clydebank Tidy; it was designed to go around the local schools and nursery schools in the area to teach them about not littering and keeping their area clean. We had a puppet show that consisted of four puppets in a large trunk basically with a scenery painted on the high back of it. There was Dirty Den (BOO), Tidy Tiger (YEAH), PC Plod (YEAH) and for the life of me I cannot remember the fourth. We also had a clown called Kleeno who ran the show and introduced the puppets, the best job I ever had, I loved it. One show we went to at the Auchentoshan School was memorable, it is a special school and occupational centre for handicapped children.

We had a room full of children who varied in physical age and mental age, and as I was getting ready as Kleeno behind the puppet show some of the kids were obviously looking out of the window because I heard a voice shout clear as a bell that it was fucking pishing outside. I could not stop laughing and tears were running down my cheeks, spoiling my make-up. It took me a bit longer than normal, but I really couldn't stop laughing. When I went out, I was introducing myself and giggling and when I looked around all the teachers were in hysterics. I eventually got started and asked the kids if they wanted to meet the puppets. Well, what a diverse response some kids shuffled back and some were happy to come up however on the way up the same voice comes again, there no real fucking puppets, by this time all the adults were in doubled up mode including me and the 3 girls and boy in the puppet show. The lad who shouted was quite tall and as he got to the first puppet, he held onto it and got his teeth right into it and I think it was Kathleen screamed and jumped up. Now there is only one response available from the young lad and it had to be told you they weren't real fucking puppets!!! This was my favourite day as Kleeno and Kathleen's possibly first tetanus injection.

Now the song:

> Keep Clydebank Tidy
> Keep Clydebank Clean
> Keep Clydebank just the nicest place you've ever seen.
> If you're driving in your car with windows open wide
> Don't think of ever throwing anything outside
> Find a bin, find a bin, find a bin and put it in
> If you go into a shop and you buy a sticky sweet
> Don't take the wrapper off and throw it in the street.
> Find a bin, find a bin, find a bin and put it in.

I am sure you will all be singing this from now on, the tune comes with the words when you start singing them. Think there was another verse but leave it at that as I think it will take you long enough to learn this.

The project only lasted eighteen months and after another short stint of unemployment I got a job at a famous Glasgow Institution called Fyfe and McGrouther. They were suppliers of all sorts of tools, ironmongery, electrical, janitorial and some building supplies as well. They had eleven different departments, and I got a job in the tool department in the office of three people, John the department manager, Ian who did all the pricing and myself to support incoming calls and assist the counter staff when required. Pricing was done via a very big pricing book with all the manufacturers sections with all their tools in there as well. Ian would get the previous day's lines and price them; he would basically take most of the day to do these and then they went along to the office for typing up for invoicing. Ian played in a famous band called the Las Vegas Showband and played some very tasty gigs. One he did was for the Jackie Stewart Shoot which used to take place I think at Gleneagles and there were many famous people attending including Sportspersons, Actors and even Royalty. Ian had his head in the clouds most of the day. When Ian was away for holiday John asked me to do the pricing and I made up a desk chart with all the main tools that went into toolkits to make it easy rather than looking them up all the time. When the lines came through I had them done by 9.30am, dreamer nothing but a dreamer, nice guy though.

We had a work night out in July 1990 for the Glasgow Fair which was when all the big factories and businesses closed for a two-week holiday. I had got to say hello to the girls in the office, but they were at the other end of the building (For those that have seen Still Game it was the big white building in the background as you walk up the stairs from Naveed's shop) so no real contact. It used to be the guys would all sit together, and the girls would do the same until a certain time in the evening, nobody knows what that time was but the mingling starts. Someone mentioned that one of the girls Susanne's brother Eddie had been knocked down coming from school and had been taken to hospital. She came in while I was up doing a stint on the decks after asking the DJ, the song was the Only Way Is Up by Yazz and the Plastic Population. I went over and asked how her brother was and she told me he would be fine, and we spoke for a while.

A month or so later I met her in the big hall at work, just after I had asked someone walking through there what they were doing in this part of the building as it was private only to be met with the words I own this place, that was the first and last time I met Campbell Graham. I asked Susanne out and we decided we would meet after work one night and go for a couple of drinks. We agreed to meet at the phone boxes at the University. Well, how was I to know there were two sets of phone boxes at the University, she was in Parliamentary Road, and I was in George Street, I waited and waited and started to think I had been stood up when I saw Susanne storming into the pub we were going too. I went in after her and she thought I had been taking the mickey out of her, but the night ended well and still to this day we are together.

The first time I met Susanne's mum was when I was out for lunch and walking along Sauchiehall Street, Susanne and mum were standing in a doorway having their lunch out of the rain. The second time I met Susanne's mum was a slightly different story, after work one Tuesday Susanne, Graham and I went to the Hurdy Gurdy Pub just round the corner from the work, Graham was going to Motherwell to watch Rangers with his scarf in his pocket and I was going to play pool in the Celtic Club in Springburn near where Susanne stayed in the Red Road flats. All three of us ended up in the Celtic Club, Graham with his scarf in his pocket and me putting myself on last at the pool hoping they wouldn't need me if they won early. We had a few drinks when I got the shout Terry you're on, it was a draw and I had to play the last game, I won the game but have to admit I do not remember one thing about the actual game. I phoned Susanne at work to be told she wasn't well and wouldn't be in today. I made my way to her house around lunchtime, and she was still in her bed when mum opened the door. I went in and suggested a wee curer might be the answer and around half an hour later there we were Susanne, Susanne's mum, and I in the Broomfield Tavern. We stayed all afternoon and into the night and Susanne's dad seemingly gave mum a rollicking as his dinner wasn't ready when he came in from work.

The first time I went to Susanne's for Sunday dinner was very interesting as well as being very full of food. Susanne had been at a recent family wedding and she put the video on and started to explain that the bride was her cousin and after watching around ten minutes of the video I piped up so the bride is your cousin is it well let me tell you that the groom is my cousin John Heron, the family were flabbergasted to this news and actually so was I.

The Pot Black pub was in Anderston Bus Station and was also in the Red-Light district of Glasgow at that time. The girls used to come into the pub for drinks and sometimes food if they had a good day, most of them also liked a game of pool so we got to know them all by name, some of them were actually very good pool players too. The first time I took Susanne back to my place we had to walk through the Red-Light District, and she was gobsmacked as a lot of the girls were saying hi Terry how are you tonight. I hadn't thought that one through, but sure Susanne was okay with my explanation.

We used to have a major pool tournament on A Saturday that started around two and sometimes would not finish until late into the night, it attracted most of the good pool players from Glasgow but also surrounding areas. Players like former world champion Ross McInnes, Mick McGoldrick, Charlie Shaw, Martin Shades who ran the pub and many more. I used to do well in the early rounds but as the night wore on so did the alcohol, most of the players mentioned and lots more would only drink soft drinks so had a head start on my stability.

The flat I was in was four floors up overlooking the Kingston Bridge. It was okay but very draughty from the old steel windows. I tried to get the council out to fix them, but they said they didn't employ blacksmiths anymore. I asked them to come and fit draught excluders on the windows and veranda door as that was where most of the draft came from however returning from work one day, I noticed something on the outside of the front door and yes they had put the draught excluder on the outside of the door. This prompted the first of many cheeky letters that I have written to various authorities over the years and this one was a complaint about the correct work being done with a reference to how delighted I was that the Council had stopped the draft escaping from the house and that other tenants would not suffer any excess coldness coming out of my place. Nothing ever happened so I just blocked the gaps where I could, did make a bit of a difference.

There was no shower in the place, so it was bath's all the time. Over the bath was a drying pulley with four wooden spars in a metal frame. (Picture for those that do not know this contraption. I got brought up with one of these in our kitchen and I knew you pulled it down, put your washing on it then pulled it up to dry. Well, my one had no rope, so I used to take the spars out and get in the bath. One day Susanne came in as I was getting the bath ready and started taking the spars out, she questioned my logic, strange woman I thought. Next minute she leans over the bath, pulls out a little knot on the end of the frame and proceeds to raise the pulley complete with spars. What a genius I thought, we had an old model where you tied the rope around the frame, and to me this was a real advancement in technology.

The heating system was air blowing through vents from a shaft that ran the whole height of the building, when the wind blew heavy which, it did the pilot light would blow out I kept trying to light it but to no avail and I had to call the Gas company to come out, the guy lit it in seconds with a blow torch. So, the next day at work I bought a blow torch, not the same quality as the Gas Company one but one I think would work. It was in the boot of the car for a while and a couple of weeks later the pilot went out, down to the car I went and got it out from under a pile of other stuff. It had a spout on it with a pattern around the edge attached to the spout, I lit the little beauty and turned it on its side to fit in and lo and behold it went all over my hand, the thing was leaking. I managed to run the short distance to the kitchen sink and put it in there still lit at the spout and around the body, mind in gear use water, turn on tap WHOOSH no not water, damp cloth, WHOOSH nope not damp cloth, aha just let it burn itself out not a big canister. I stood back in the doorway to keep an eye on it and BANG as it went I turned away and shards of metal were at the far end of the living room and the label had decorated the door frame around me but I had not been touched by one bit of it, how I do not know but after I stopped shaking I walked over to the sink only to see a large hole. Susanne came in that night, and she was astounded that I had been uninjured with the mess that was around.

I went to the council and although I had been in the flat for a few weeks, I told them that was the first time I had noticed the big hole in the sink as I had been working away, great result with a brand-new kitchen sink and unit.

At Christmas time in Fyfe and McGrouther customers used to hand in gifts of vouchers and bottles of spirits, I thought it was great our department got £400 worth of vouchers for Haddow's the off sales company and plenty of bottles. Just before Christmas break up for holiday, we were called to the office one by one and the directors were there, all except my mate Campbell. I was told how well I had done throughout the year and how profitable the company was, and they handed me a brown envelope with a half bottle of whisky in it. I questioned them about the profitability and the company's generosity to employees who had worked very hard. It was frowned on answering back to them and I got some real dirty looks. This was the beginning of the end but better was to follow. We all went to the Hurdy Gurdy for a while and then Graham and I decided we would go into town and then get the bus home. When we got to the top of the stairs (Where Naveed's shop is) I stopped and said to Graham a ½ bottle for a year's work, I turned around and as said before it was a large building and had scaffolding up as well and I launched the brown envelope at the building, I heard it crash a window somewhere to the right. I was due back to work on the 3rd of January but didn't make it until the 5th and when I walked into the office there was a very strong smell of whisky, I wasn't aiming for any window but managed to get my own office. There was a bookcase in front of the window so seemingly it took them a while to find out where it came from, but they pulled the bookcase away and found a brown envelope. Luckily there were no names on them, but I was called along to the Directors office where I promptly denied all knowledge. I left a couple of days later; the vouchers had been used to buy all the half bottles miserable bastards.

We had been out at a party one Friday night and early Saturday morning the door chapped and it was the neighbour downstairs who told me I was flooding him in the kitchen cupboard, strange set up in these flats as the cistern for the toilet pan was in that cupboard, I went and looked and sure enough it was overflowing. I phoned the Council emergency services and a plumber came in around a couple of hours, I had switched the water off so as not to cause any more damage. A tall guy with slightly ginger hair and beard came out, he could nearly reach the cistern, but I got him a chair to stand on, he said it is your ball cock mate it is jammed, he moved it around and said he adjusted it and should be fine. Two weeks later on the Saturday afternoon Susanne and I came home from a shopping trip, we had only been out a couple of hours and when we got off the lift there were Police and workers outside the flat, we went in and there was around six inches deep water all over the house, yes the ball cock had jammed again, I had went to the toilet before I left. In the long cupboards we had all my LP's and all the covers were destroyed by the water, so I put a claim for £1500 into the Council not just for the records but furniture and shoes were all damaged and they came back with a rejection of the claim. I objected and they told me the reason they had rejected was that they had no record of the plumber being out the first time, I described the guy, told them I could go to their Darnick Street site and pick him out, but they weren't having it, simply they had no record. I went to a lawyer who advised me to notify them I was withholding the rent and to put it in the bank to pay when the case ended. I did it for a good few months and it was at this time that Susanne and I decided we would buy a house and move in together, the rent money we saved came in handy.

I used to do the discos in the Pot Black at the weekends and there were some good nights, we even had a couple of nights where Radio Clyde DJ's would come in and do a night. One of the barmen Pat had moved away and was running a pub in Maryhill in Glasgow, he asked me to do a night for him and I agreed not really knowing what it was for but turned up and set up along with Susanne. The people started to arrive, and I noted that there were a lot of young guys all wearing white shirts and black trousers carrying plastic bags. The guy who was running the party asked me to play three records when they were requested. All the young guys left and came back in wearing dark glasses and berets and marching to the first two of the songs, however the third was a disaster as it was a single record normally played at 45RPM but this one was to be played at 33RPM and it played way too fast until I realised and corrected, some very strange looks indeed. I had now completed my first fundraising disco for a sectarian group. Pat moved on to a pub at the docks in Port Glasgow, which is a real rough house area, he assured me nothing like last one and to incorporate a bit of a quiz. I told him we would bring gear in the afternoon and set up for evening Sunday night session. Susanne opened the door as I was carrying equipment just as the guy got smacked with the pool cue and split open his jaw. Pat was standing there, and he said it was never like this normally. We set up and left to come back later. When we walked in it was packed and was so noisy, the women were worse than the men. I started the disco and the guy with the split jaw came up and asked Susanne to dance but she refused saying she wasn't allowed by her boss looking at me. I'll smash his c—t in if he doesn't let you dance, Pat intervened and off he went. Looking around I decided that the quiz would have to be downgraded to a simpler range of questions to accommodate the audience. First question was who Popeye's girlfriend is and no one could answer, out of about 70 people not one knew.

Another disco I done was in a pub near Parkhead in Glasgow and was probably my first encounter with someone seriously on the drugs. Susanne and mum came along for the night, first request comes from the drugged-up guy, and he asked for Sweet Caroline by Neil Diamond, I said I would play it soon and he said play it now, wow this disco game was getting tough, so I played it. Five minutes later he asks if I have Sweet Caroline and to play it, I protested but in vain as he was adamant, he hadn't heard it the first time. Nobody else seemed bothered and after the twentieth and final rendition of Sweet Caroline it was time to pack up and there was Susanne, mum and I grabbing everything and getting out of there as fast as we could.

My last disco using my own gear was a five night stint for a works Xmas parties at a place called Lodge on the Loch at Loch Lomond. The lady who ran the place said she was not that keen on discos as she had only recently had a wedding, the DJ turned up late and left early but I assured her this would not happen. I went on the Thursday and set up all the gear and tested and all good. Next day was my works Xmas party near London and I was booked on the 6.00pm flight and would be back for 8.00pm start of the disco as agreed. Well you have probably guessed this and yes the flight was delayed for an hour and I did not arrive until 8.45pm. I was talking to Susanne keeping her up to date and she was keeping the lady informed. I did get there and started right away, turns out I knew some of the people there that night and they gave me a rough time for holding up their party. Next four nights all go smoothly and the last night into Xmas day I played Loch Lomond by Runrig and announced that this was my last disco as it couldn't get any better playing Loch Lomond on the banks of Loch Lomond, job done.

We were working hard, I had joined a company called RD Taylor as inside sales and I was doing discos for a guy called Robert Johnson, I would take my records and he supplied the gear, Susanne was still in Fyfe and McGrouther and she had taken a part time job in Haddow's. The disco thing went pear shaped when I had a couple of gigs which really threw me. I was at the Pitz in Paisley for a charity night organised by Radio Clyde thinking maybe there was a chance to get noticed however I did get noticed but not for the right reasons. The place had a small stage, and the floor was wooden and every time someone came near the stage the records jumped and of course there were people coming to the stage for fun even though I had asked them not to and after about ninety minutes I gave up and left. Not a great experience but worse was to follow on Christmas Eve.

I was booked to do the night at The Horseshoe Bar in Glasgow City Centre, it is a very famous pub as it had the longest bar in the UK. Anyway, people finishing work heading for the Horseshoe to start their holidays and festivities, place bouncing and DJ Terry raring to go. Get the Xmas songs on right away and everyone up dancing wherever they could, in the first hour I had got them. Just after the hour Oh I wish it could be Xmas every…………..nothing, total silence. Switch everything off, strip the gear back, leave for ten minutes, and switch on daaaay…………nothing. Tried a few times but the decks were constantly overheating. I left after that and decided Robert Johnson and I were no more.

I decided to get into the pub quizzes as they were very popular and generally during the week. I was at one and I had a chat with the quizmaster, and he gave me the name of the guy who produced them and supplied them to quizmasters for the pubs he had set up. I got in touch with Barry Hanniford (Won quarter of a million on who wants to be a millionaire) and he suggested I come to his unit in Rutherglen which I did. When I was sitting there, he shouted to his partner to come in and who walks in but Robert Johnson!!! He said do I know you and I said no I don't think so as I had only ever met him once when I started doing his discos.

When I started the quizzes, it meant we had five jobs between us and the deposit for the house was close.

I did the quizzes for several years in various pubs and clubs throughout Glasgow and surrounding areas but by far the best was Grier's pub in Easterhouse where I used to do a Tuesday. Easterhouse was a deprived area, and the quiz nights were well supported initially, but when the questions were too difficult people lost interest and the same team won every week. Barry's quizzes were very good but for Easterhouse maybe not, so I suggested to the manager that I do them myself, I changed the format to make the first ten questions multiple choice and after that round nearly everyone was on the same score with creative marking. Round two were mainly sporting questions which everyone was clued up on so again after 20 questions the scores were close. Round three was a bit more difficult but with a few hints from the quizmaster to certain teams it was still close after 29 questions. The last question was who I am or what am I for 12 points, starting at 12 and then minus two for every clue, I would take turns dropping hints and sometimes answers to a different team each Tuesday. The good team still won a lot of the times, but you should have seen the delight on the faces of the other teams when it was their turn to win. Was it cheating, YES did it bring joy and some form of equality to people YES was Bob the local priest involved YES (Father Bob enjoyed a beer and a quiz and was a Rangers supporter). There was a guy I got quite friendly with in there called John the ex-fireman and he told me one of the funniest true stories I have ever heard. He was sitting in with his wife one Saturday when he suddenly felt pains across his chest, a heart attack surely, he thought, his wife got the ambulance and off they went to the hospital with the pains getting worse. They hooked him up to the ECG units and started doing tests and after about 20 minutes the nurse came and gave him a couple of tablets, two minutes later John was farting like a trooper and this treatment saved his life, thank God for Peppermint tablets. The doctor did say though that he had done the right thing because you never know, thanks John.

RD Taylor based in Glasgow were distributors for many different companies like Dow Corning, 3M, Loctite, Multicore Solders and Electrolube to do with adhesives, sealants, and chemicals My job was inside sales, and I was support for the external sales rep Ken Robertson (remember that name). Our big customers were the Ministry of Defence and the Electronics sector, which was booming at the time with IBM, Motorola, NEC and many more coming to Scotland. We had a great team there and some great teamwork had to happen when we got orders from the Ministry of Defence for one hundred thousand tubes of Dow Corning 732 Sealant which came in Clear, White and Black. These orders would come in and we would get the stock ordered and delivered to the Ibrox site then with military precision we would order Pizza and Beer and set about the task in hand. Each box contained 100 tubes, 10 boxes of 10 which were individually boxed and a tube of 732 inside, all had to be labelled which was 211 labels per box. We had a production line going and drinking beer and eating pizza as we went, this was all done after hours over a few nights. Because I had a knack for attention to detail not sure where that came from, but I got involved in dealing with export customers. These included the Royal Navy Mazagon Dock in India, Mohammad Haddad in Kuwait and sending products directly to a company in Libya. The company in Libya used to order Ciba Geigy (Araldite products) by the pallets, the paperwork had to be very precise as the hardener in these kits was very volatile. There was a British company who got into trouble for selling certain types of pipes into this country and I am sure they were fined or shut down. One day I get a telephone call from someone in government asking for me personally, I immediately put it onto my boss, and it turns out the hardener they reckoned was being used as part of an explosives set up and we had to stop selling it, in fact I think that was around the time the government started the trade embargo with Libya. Three months later we got an enquiry for the same products in the same quantities from a company in Malta, I asked boss man Bill what to do and he replied send it which we did, I think I know where it ended up.

I was seconded to Aberdeen branch for a few weeks to cover for holidays coming home at the weekend, one weekend Susanne decided to come up instead and we stayed at the Holiday Inn instead of the crap place I stayed in during the week. We went out for a tour around Aberdeen on the Saturday afternoon visiting watering holes along the way, well afternoon turned into night and then late night. We decided to get a Kebab with a nice bright red sauce to take back to the room, the Holiday Inn do not have any cutlery or plates in their rooms so we went back downstairs where there was a private party going on and we helped ourselves to a couple of plates and cutlery. We went back upstairs switched on the TV and the movie Ghost was on so we thought a good idea would be to put the pillows up the other end of the bed, eat the kebab and watch the movie. We would have been lucky if we each lasted five minutes awake and the next thing was the maid coming into the room in the morning, we did manage to waken and stop her which was just as well because the bed looked like there had been a murder committed on it with Kebab and sauce all over the pillows and bed. We did clean up best we could and it didn't look to bad after hiding what we could.

Ken Robertson the external sales rep handed in his notice and was going to join Electrolube one of our suppliers so I asked if I could get his job which I did get, yes out on the road with Ken's company car.

One day I was looking for something in the warehouse when a bulging folder fell off the shelf. I asked what all these very fat folders were, and it was official order confirmations from GEC. We used to deal with 11 GEC sites in Scotland and they spent lots of money with us. Their ordering process was they would send a fax for the products required, then they would send a confirmation order with around 20 pages of terms and conditions for every order which could be in the hundreds every month and I considered it nuts and not environmentally friendly. I went to see the procurement manager at GEC Marconi at Hillend in Fife and suggested that they sent the fax, we sent the goods and at the end of the month I sat down with procurement and went through everything that had been ordered and delivered then they would raise one main order for goods for the month. Well, I don't think I have had my hand shaken so rigorously in all my life. He took it to the board and from the start of the next month it was rolled out, not only that they told the other ten sites, and it was adopted as well. Now that was a win/win if ever I saw one. It snowballed from there because they wanted us to buy everything for them from existing suppliers, basically they would get a quote from a supplier and send it to us and we would put 15% on it and buy it from the supplier. Some of these suppliers were competitors to us but GEC told them if they did not supply through RD Taylor then they would find another product to put on their drawings.

Bill the man gave me a week in his Villa in Calahonda, Mijas Costa Spain for this work and this was the first time I had been abroad and second time flying, my first time on a plane was not until I was 32 on a weekend trip to London. We went with friends, and she paid for everything, we never spent a penny. She told us she had been doing that well at her job and making huge bonus and that her boss had paid for the hotel and flights, so every meal every drink was accounted for. 6 months after that she received a two-and-a-half-year prison sentence for fraud, thank you my friend for a wonderful weekend.

I had built up a great reputation with Ken's customers over the phone so when I went to see them, I was very well received and in fact a natural salesperson with a swivel head, everywhere I went I found products that we could supply that Ken had never even found or mentioned. Bill gave me another week at the Villa for the great results.

We were very big distributors for Multicore solders at this time, but they were going through a phase of taking big accounts direct from us saying they were too big for us, we serviced these accounts well and never let any of them down, it was all about more profit for the big boys as these products were specified on drawings. Some of these accounts were mine like OKI and Honeywell and I was peed off. I came across a company called Warton Metals who were a start-up company based in Hornsea

TERRY DUFF (WEE GLASGOW GUY)

Yorkshire who had some good new technology solder wires, but Bill didn't want to look at them as he didn't want to upset the current supplier, yes, the one who was taking away all our business. So, I spoke with Warton Metals, and I left RD Taylor and joined them. I was the rep for Scotland, England, Wales and Ireland basically I was the guy. I was doing well and had managed to secure business from some of the bigger guys because of the reduced fume content of the Warton Wires. Nokia, Panasonic, Honeywell and many more big businesses were coming along too. I had a trip to Ireland booked with the Irish Distributor to visit sites across there. On the trip we went to Galway it was the night of the Rugby World Cup semi-final and we went to the pub to watch it, we left around 10.00pm because we had a customer visit at 9.00am the next morning. We met with the production manager at Applied Power Conversions, he was dressed in dungarees with turn ups to his shins and one of the coolest guys I had met in business. He had obviously been out watching the rugby, all night by the look of it, we talked about the rugby and then he said he had to go for breakfast. We went to the canteen, Dave and I already had breakfast, so we just had drinks, he came back with a huge fry up and a huge glass of milk. We got talking about business and he went to have a drink of milk and spilled the whole lot in his breakfast, undeterred he kept saying it was all going the one way anyway. He took us into the office, gave us what they were buying, and quantities and price and we went away and sent him a quote and he started buying the next week, a great visit. Another great visit was with a company who had a small factory on the banks of Loch Ness. We sat outside drinking tea and looking up the Loch, cool. Warton employed a new rep from Kent to look after the south of the country which made sense, his second name was Yeo and there was a Tory politician of that name at the time. I met him in the Victoria Hotel in Hornsea got talking and he asked where I was from and I said Glasgow in Scotland and he replied oh yes the testing ground in reference to Maggie Thatcher's Poll Tax for Scotland first before the rest of the country, after Chris picked him up I got the feeling that Warton Metals was no longer for me but I did stay a little while longer.

We had bought a house in Moodiesburn just on the outskirts of Glasgow and moved in September 1993, it was a two-bedroom bungalow with a huge, tiered back garden which we loved. It was the Glasgow Fair and I had decided to take a week's holiday, I drove back the five hours from Hornsea on the Friday, getting home around 9.30pm just when the phone rang. It was Susanne's brother Eddie and he asked me if I would like to go and see the Rolling Stones, not their biggest fan but thought good to see them, when? Sunday night. Whereabouts? Wembley, What? Yeah, we have tickets and a car to get us there and back. Eddie worked for Volkswagon part sponsors of the event, and they had four tickets and had given Eddie and another guy in his work a car to get us there. We set off late Saturday night and got to Wembley around 11.00am with Eddie and the other guy sharing the driving. The gates opened at 12.00pm and the couple we were with said they were going in and when I heard the first band were on at 4.00pm I headed for the pub with Eddie who had two shandies. Turns out the supporting act didn't get on because of thunder and lightning and power cuts but the Stones came on about 8.00pm and were excellent. We left right after the concert finished and on the road for around 11.00pm and back home in Glasgow early Monday morning. A bloody long weekend driving but worthwhile, thanks Eddie.

Right at the back of our house was the Nights of St Columba's social club and they had a cabaret on one night featuring the Drifters, one of the originals was still around using the name. The first half of the show was great and when I went to the toilet there was a queue for the urinal and just in front of me was a Drifter. As you know there is a long held thought about coloured men and the size of their manhood. The place was still busy when I said to him alright big fella, whip it out and let's see it, he just started laughing as did everyone else in the toilet but we never got sight of it and after washing our hands he shook mine and I told him for the rest of my life I would tell people that I had pissed with a Drifter.

On a business trip to Cologne, heading home on the Friday around lunchtime we left going to Kent where I had left my car at one of the team's houses. I started the drive back to Glasgow but started getting tired and decided to book into one of the service station motels, first one full so had a cup of tea and a power nap and then onwards. I stopped off at another three to no avail and was reminded that the British Open golf was on at Royal Troon and people were making their way there as well as other travellers. I stopped a good few times and eventually got into the driveway around three in the morning with no keys, no problem Susanne and mum were home and they were absolutely out of the game. I tried doors, windows banging and shouting and nothing. I ended up sleeping in the car and when mum got up to make a cup of tea, she noticed the car in the driveway and opened the door for me. An eventful and exceptionally long trip home.

Another occasion I was golfing on the Friday at Deer Park Golf Club Livingston, and we were having a dinner afterwards, so we were all booked into the hotel there. I left there Saturday late morning, and it was a beautiful day so decided on the way home to stop and buy a barbecue and plans to invite people for Sunday lunch. Sunday up early and it is pissing it down with rain and it stayed on all day, so the barbecue was transferred to the loft where it remained until two years ago when Eddie brought it down and gave us it back still unused some 25 years later. Eddie had moved into the house when we went overseas.

I had decided to join a local golf club, but some had waiting lists, and I eventually went to Langlands in East Kilbride miles away, but a mate of mine Peter Campbell played there so made it easier to fit in and we had some great laughs there. After playing on a Saturday, we would watch the racing and have a game where the twelve of us would put £1 in each and pick a horse and the winner would get the money if not one a rollover was declared. The slight problem with this which made it more fun was that only a handful of races had 12 runners meaning a winner was certain. In the summer some of the fields could be up to 30 runners which meant 18 of the horses were against us and in the winter there might only be four runners so eight people wouldn't have a runner, there was some very big winnings to be had on a Saturday and now and then it would carry on to the following week.

Peter and his co-directors Albert and Steven and I had a day out in between Xmas and New Year and settled on a game of snooker at a club in Rutherglen which was run by a friend from the Pot Black Martin. To say it was cold was the biggest understatement of the century. We played with our coats on even though heating was on. We left around 5.00pm and went for a Chinese meal after that and after a phone call we were headed for Shawfield greyhound stadium but not before a visit to the off sales for four half bottles of vodka. Into stadium and order two cans of coke and two cans of Irn Bru as mixers for the vodka. We were last out singing walking in a winter wonderland and straight across to Joe McBride's (former Celtic legend) pub across the road to continue the party. We left the pub with the intention of getting two taxis, one for Peter and Steven heading north and one for Albert and me going south. I may have mentioned it was very cold in the afternoon while by 12.30am it was extremely bitter and the more we waited for the taxis the more we were getting closer together for the heat. We waited around for about twenty minutes and when a taxi came we all bundled in. Peter was first out in East Kilbride, Steven next in Hamilton, me next in Moodiesburn and poor Albert last out in Bearsden with no money and he had to waken his wife to pay the £55 taxi fare. Next day I saw that the temperature with wind chill had reached -22c.

One time I was playing in the club championship against a guy of a four handicap, I was playing off 14 at the time so had 10 shots off him. The boys said they would come out and watch the later holes and that I might be back in before they got out. First hole parred but I get a shot so 1 up, second hole par, and I get a shot two up, 3rd hole I birdie and go three up, 4th hole halved, 5th hole both par and I get a shot and I go four up after five holes. Next tee I go straight down the middle he pulls it left into the trees and the driver goes flying for miles also into the trees, as he heads left, I turn away and head back to the clubhouse where all the guys are thinking I have been slaughtered. Here he come's storming in asking what the hell is going on, I tell him I play golf to win but to have fun and throwing clubs is not what I want to see as I had seen someone get a real sore face from that action in the past. He tries to give me the tie, but I am adamant that he is the winner and I had signed his card already, red faced and tail between his legs he leaves, and the guys are all going nuts and screaming their heads off as they had never seen anything like that before.

My last game of golf at Langlands was also memorable as it was the weekend before I was going to Australia. At the 9th hole one of the playing partners has his three wood out on the fairway and I am a bit ahead of him, he slices it and smacks me right in the small of my back and I end up on the plane with a bruised back with a white middle and along with the hand trapped in the door incident I was lucky to make it out of the UK. When I left to go to Australia I lost touch with Peter until 25th January 2024 when I was involved in a trade day at one of my customers and got talking to Stuart one of the exhibitors who told me he came from East Kilbride. I told him I played golf at Langland's and he told me his father in law Peter Campbell played there, the hairs on my back stood up. I got his number and called him asking how he was, was he still golfing, enjoying your retirement and how was Carol. I then asked him if he knew who was talking too and he never had a clue but was very surprised when I told him and we are arranging a catch up soon.

Susanne and I went on a few good holidays which we deserved and once a year for a few years we made it a family one with Susanne's mum, brother Eddie, Cheryl and a friend for company and my brother John. Every person we saw or met used to get a nickname, but John came up with the classic when a guy walking down the street in only swimming trunks and trainers got the famous PANTYMAN, we were all in hysterics. For some reason I used to be merry when going home from these events and had a few separate scenarios that might not go down too well nowadays. One was a mask I had of the fantastic Les Ferdinand who most will know as an ex-footballer with dark skin, I put it on while in the queue at the airport and the attendant freaked when she looked from my passport, but she did see the funny side. Another was when a little baby crawling around the floor and I started following him doing the same thing, every time he looked round, he and the whole airport including police and security were in hysterics. Another time I lost a sandal, don't know where don't know when. When I got to the airport someone said to me you only have one sandal on and I corrected them by saying I only had one sandal off! This happened a few times until I think people got fed up. Another one to follow on a trip from Vanuatu to Sydney. Susanne, mum, and I went for a ten-day holiday to Malta, I had been doing a lot of travelling and was really looking forward to it. I sometimes suffer from hard wax in my ears which can get uncomfortable when flying so used some drops to soften them. On the plane I fell asleep, and Susanne wakened me when we got to Malta, on the bus to the resort I fell asleep again and when we got into the apartment I went straight to bed. At some point Susanne and mum looked in and there was a cat lying in between my legs and they screamed, and I never heard a thing. I wakened next day and had to go to the doctors as the pain in my ears was unbearable. It turns out I had used old ear drops and had poisoned both ears and was on antibiotics for the time I was there. The doctor told me I could have beer but best to stay off the spirits. I did for the first week and was feeling much better. We went out and within a couple of hours I have grabbed a Geordie girl and we are doing you're the one that I want on the Karaoke, then I am out on the street following people and trying to get them into the pub still with the microphone, I was doing okay until Susanne wisely intervened and took me home.

The week away from Warton Metals turned out to be the change in my life that I never expected. Ken Robertson had moved on from being the Scotland and North of

England rep with Electrolube to European Sales. I heard late on in the process, and they had offered the job to someone but if they did not accept, they would get in touch.

On the Tuesday night I went to see the old gang in Grier's for quiz night and had a good time. I got a taxi home and when I got in Susanne asks did you check the mail, yup, did you check the answering machine, yup, did you check the fax, nope, turns out there was a fax from Electrolube inviting me for an interview which had fallen down the back of the machine, the guy they offered the job too had turned it down.

I flew down to Heathrow and had breakfast on the plane including a yoghurt which had a mind of its own when I opened it, it went everywhere, shirt and tie, I managed to rub these enough to make them not so noticcable. When I met Liz, she said I should wipe the yoghurt off my face, great start to an interview. It went well and I was offered the job which I duly accepted, the second following of Ken Robertson. On the way back in the British Midland flight magazine I read a bit from a book, it was by comedian Tony Hawks and called around Ireland with a fridge, I got the book, and I can say it is a great read and I have done so many times.

Part of the job induction involved me going out with some of the existing team of reps, one of these was Mike who looked after Southwest England and Wales. He set up a meeting with Panasonic engineering team, a couple who I had met with when I was at Warton Metals but this one was different. I walked into the room with Mike and around a dozen engineers and after Mike introduced me, they started having the meeting in WELSH. They then all burst out laughing and told me that Mike had set this up, nice one. Another visit was with Paul whose nickname was Barney, he told me the story of how it came about. Paul did look a lot like Fred Flintstone however one night in a pub this guy said he looked like the guy of the Flintstone's and proceeded to call him Barney, stuck with him and another lovely fella.

The job was going very well, and I was looking to take on a new distributor based in Hull called Grosvenor Associates, one of the guys there was Ross who I had met at Warton, and he had left to go there. It was a difficult start as Ross wanted to place a stock order, but we would only give them a £1000 credit limit, he very nearly quit and went elsewhere but we persevered and through time Grosvenor became Electrolube's third biggest customer behind two huge multi nationals.

Ross owned a few racehorses and a couple turned out to be very good and won some good races and were placed in high class races. El Astronaute and Safe Voyage were favourites of racegoers and during the pandemic Ross appeared on the ITV racing programme quite a few times from his office with his staff and was good entertainment. His first horse was one called the Wow

Signal won a maiden race at Ayr by nine lengths and was promptly sold to a big international group. He went on to win a Group 2 at Ascot, a Group 1 at Deauville and then ran last at Longchamp and was retired to stud.

Ken Robertson had been transferred again this time to work in Sydney under a lovely guy Andrew that I met at an event we had down In Leicester and I got on well with him for the week. I wasn't interested in moving down south for the European role, so Ken's shadow was safe for a while.

I had a new boss Adrian Hanrahan who was an Irish guy and again I got on well with him and we went on joint visits one day in Newcastle around about October time in 1998. We went to visit a few customers and he reacted by telling me I had a great relationship with my customers and where would I be with the company in three years' time. Well I had been talking to Ross about joining his company so my reply was I probably wouldn't be with the company unless it was in Australia as I had to keep following Ken Robertson (remember him) and one of my best mates had emigrated there too. Stevie used to send me letters with these beautiful pictures of the family and the beach, one day I had a beer with his dad and I said can you tell Stevie to stop sending me these letters and pictures as he is depressing me. I asked Bill his dad when he was going to visit and he said never, if I go, I go once and stay, his wife Ina was there a lot. They both emigrated together, and Bill was true to his word, a wonderful family.

It was the day before my 40th birthday or the day after that I got the call to say that Ken Robertson had resigned his post in Sydney and what did I want to do about it knowing that neither big boss Gerald Kingsbury or Adrian wanted me to go but I said I would like to go and see it and that they would arrange it later.

My 40th birthday was held over two nights, a night in the Pot Black to which the family had ordered me a Bertha Gram, an outsize lady who sits on your knee. In walks the Bertha Gram and she bursts out laughing as I did too, the rest of the party are wondering what is going on and I tell them I have known this woman twenty-five years, Evelyn was a dear friend and best friend to a previous girlfriend of mine going back to end of school days. The other part of my birthday was at Shawfield Greyhound Stadium on Saturday, and it was a great night as I think I also got four or five winners. Please watch out for fiftieth and sixtieth birthdays please, following later obviously.

40th Pot Black and dogs Billy, Stuart, Mark, Palmy, Bud, Me and Gordon, Eddie, Henry, Angela, Nicky, Mum, Sus, Ann Marie and Tam

Mid-February I left Glasgow in the snow and landed in Sydney in the blazing sunshine. I was picked up by the guy who would be my new boss Kerry Thomas a Kiwi and taken to the branch in Brookvale on the Northern Beaches (Does that sound good or what?). The third following of Ken Robertson.

I stay at Kerry's for the first couple of nights, but he lives in Kenthurst well away from the beaches, I ask to stay nearer the beach, and he tells me that is not in the budget, but I did get my wish in the cheapest place on the Northern Beaches, alarm bells ringing for me here. One of my first jobs for the week is to talk to a customer who is threatening to sue us for $150,000, he had put the athlete statues around the CenterPoint Tower in the heart of Sydney for the forthcoming Olympic Games. One thing Ken was good at was keeping paperwork. I checked back and I discovered that Ken had recommended a potting resin which would have made the unit completely watertight, but the customer had decided on using a conformal coating which gives moisture protection but is not waterproof. Lawsuit averted.

The week was great, and I enjoyed meeting the staff, seeing how things worked and touring the Northern Beaches especially some of the Golf Courses including the spectacular Long Reef Golf Club. On Saturday Kerry took me around Sydney and showed me lots of good places including Bondi. Then it was back to the grey skies of Glasgow.

I spoke with Susanne and told her about it and said I wanted to give it a go and we could make a different life for us, she was hesitant as her and mum were very close, in fact mum spent a lot of time with both of us as when we were going out mum would generally come with us, Susanne's dad didn't go out much and he sometimes worked weekends as well. Mum gave Susanne the blessing for her to go and try it out, it was a two year contract with six months' probation so not the end of the world.

I left on Friday the 12th May, Liz dropped me off at the airport and I was getting my bag out the back seat and the guy who was replacing me shut the door on my fingers, lucky enough it was an Alfa Romeo and the padding around the doors was good, no real damage done but close. I left Electrolube that day but was going to work for the parent company and they had three brands in Australia, Electrolube, AF Cleaning products and representing a Japanese soldering tool manufacturing company called Hakko. A car was left for me at the Airport, and I moved into a rental flat fifty yards from the middle surf club on Manly beach. The car was an old Mitsubishi that Kerry had for years, this was my company car and I found out he had sold it to the company for $17,000. Seriously, it was lucky if it would have fetched $5000 if sold to anyone else. The alarm bells are ringing.

I started work on Monday 15th May 1999 and on Wednesday Kerry took me to a trade show at the

Australian National University Canberra (I go back here later in the book). I could not believe it but the temperature showed in the car was -3 degrees, but it was a good day workwise and got me to see other parts of Australia in a very short space of time. Next stop was Melbourne and I stayed in a nice place this time. It was the week of the Manchester United and Bayern Munich Champions League Final. It was Thursday morning in Australia, and I set the alarm to watch it. The plan was to make a cup of tea lie in bed until halftime, go for a shower and shave and then watch the second half. Half time came and I was on the phone to Susanne, so thought just leave it get it done after the game. Getting towards the end of the game and Manchester United equalise, dive into the bathroom quick shower and shave and out for extra time. Come out and there they are running around the pitch with the trophy, I reckon I missed thirty seconds of that game and that was enough for Sir Alex's team to win the trophy.

Susanne came for a week's holiday in July, and it pissed down for the whole week. We would sit in the Steyne pub opposite the beach most days and I would ask her if she liked it yet but wasn't getting the response I wanted. We did other stuff during the week as well as went and saw some of the sights, well what we could through the rain. We went to the Blue Mountains in Western Sydney and never saw a mountain because of the fog. Nearing the end of the week we were going back to the flat and going to get a pizza from the shop around the corner when as we got near saw the guy with five pizzas in his hand locking the door, we were nearly there when a car came through the big puddle and soaked us deliberately. The pizza guy saw this and I told him we were just heading into his shop, and he gave us two pizzas for nothing. He was a very good guy.

I moved out of the flat after three months and moved to what they call a duplex in Queenscliff, a different suburb but only 200 yards away from the flat. It had wonderful views overlooking Manly Beach, it was an okay place that had a pool, but it was way up a winding set of dangerous stairs. When I lived here, I decided to try and find a golf club to join. First stop Manly Golf Club, a posh looking gentleman and lady behind the counter. I asked about joining and he said it was $7,000 to join and $7,000 per year so basically $14,000 up front, he also adds that I need to be nominated by five members who have been members for five years, easy answer to this one, mate I have only just arrived in Australia, and I don't even know five people yet!!!

I took in a lodger here to help with the rent, a South African backpacker called Tim who sometimes paid his rent and sometimes he didn't depend on the work situation, he enjoyed surfing so wasn't that keen on working. I used to stay home on a Friday and do ironing and stuff ready for work on Monday. One night when I was home alone, I saw a massive storm coming in.

I had opened the bottle of Glenmorangie that the old work had given me and sat at the breakfast bar watching, it was amazing and as it got towards Manly it turned away and started heading north. I woke up on the breakfast bar with very little left in the bottle of whisky. Tim had met an Asian girl and had taken to bringing her round on a Friday which I did explain was my night for staying in but he just ignored me and was taking the piss with the rent. He was really getting on my nerves and the next day I kicked him out.

One day while driving home I turned into the first street I had stayed in Manly Pine Street and was heading towards the beach to turn left for Queenscliff when this crazy surfer guy runs right out in front of me, top half of his wetsuit down and board in hand and I had to slam on the brakes. IDIOT Mr Goran Ivanisevic, seemingly he loved to surf when he was in Australia for the Open.

I was in the Charlton Bar in Manly one Saturday night and met a fireman called Peter and his mate, we got talking about golf and he told me they were playing in the morning at Balgowlah Golf Club at the top of Sydney Road and asked if I wanted to join them It was a nine hole course with fantastic fairways and greens and a pleasure to play. During the week I went in and met the pro Jeff and joined right away.

I had played a couple of Saturdays with Johnny who was the head greenkeeper, he was a very good player and the third week we played with a couple of new members called Adam and James which was quite weird as those were my brothers names, we ended up playing together regularly after that. Adam and James were given handicaps of 21 and 22 from memory and at the 4th hole on the first day Adam stuck his second shot two inches from the hole and James chipped his in, what was going on here as both were new golfers, but they did play Hockey together at a very high level and both played for New South Wales.

On the first day I met Adam and James, they invited me into Manly as it was the Food and Wine festival, and I met them there with Adam's wife Deb and her friend Cass. Great day and Adam invited me back to his house for a few more drinks. We were outside and I was going to the toilet and the girls were now dancing in their G strings, Adam was mortified and he went nuts shouting I bring a new guy in and you two are doing that what a disgrace. For months on end when I was anywhere near them, they were mortified, thanks girls.

Susanne was coming to stay in October along with her mum and Cheryl who were coming for a holiday, it was a great chance for them to see the sights in better weather. It was a great time Susanne's mum is a real fun-loving woman and she is bonkers into the bargain, pictures included will prove this. It was nice for Susanne to have someone to travel with and it was great to see Cheryl who I hadn't seen for five months, they had a great time for the two weeks they were there, and it was hard saying goodbye at the airport, but we had promised to go back to Scotland for Christmas and New Year so not long to wait.

We moved out of the duplex after the six-month lease was up and moved into a house with a pool in North Manly a different suburb again but this one was only five hundred yards from the duplex, crazy people with their suburbs. The previous two places were furnished, we got a settee from a colleague at work and bought a fridge and a TV, well two TV's the first one didn't have the SBS channel which was showing the Mardi Gras that night and Susanne wanted to watch it. They were second hand as was the fridge, but it got us started and the Mardi gras was good, I watched it with her to keep her company.

I had kept in touch with Ken Robertson and he invited us up to the house on the Central Coast of New South Wales, he was staying there with his girlfriend. We were there a few hours and starving when the doorbell went and it was a guy and a young girl, he was bringing her back to her mum after a parental visit. The door was ajar and I noticed it was Andrew who had left the company earlier but this was the reason Ken had left was that he was having an affair with his bosses wife.

We met Lawrence and Margaret on a holiday to a place called Arillas in Corfu, we met on the bus going to the resort and as they got off before us, we said we might catch up with you somewhere along the holiday. The next day we discovered that Arillas was a two-street town, we walked down towards the beach and bumped into them as they were walking along the beach from their accommodation. We spent the two weeks together nearly every day, we also met three girls from Edinburgh one of them Julie had booked at the last minute and left her wee boy Jamo with his dad. There was a pub that had disco gear but no DJ so I asked if I could use them, and the guy agreed. He sure knew what he was doing as when we went into the pub the first night there were around ten customers, the other three pubs were busy. The first night I performed the place was bouncing and the other pubs were a lot quieter there were even a lot of local Greeks who came along too. One day as Susanne and I were walking down towards the beach we saw an older guy looking in a shop window and he had a Celtic top on with a very famous player's name, he was a hero at Celtic before going to Barcelona and then Manchester United, have you got it yet. LARRSON, yes, he had two R's instead of two S's and we couldn't stop laughing. He came into the pub, and I offered him a drink, but he didn't drink, his name was Jimmy, and he came from Glasgow but lived in Hemel Hempstead in England. On the last day of the holiday, we had run out of money and were preparing to go on the one-hour journey into Corfu town to get the bank when Jimmy says I will give you money, save you a two hour round trip on the last day of your holiday. How nice was that he gave us money and his address to send a cheque to. When I got home a touch of mischief came over me not to send the cheque, I said to Susanne that I would never see him again but was joking. I sent Jimmy the bank cheque. A few years later I went to the Warringah Mall for my lunch and stood in the queue at the baker's when I heard the Scottish voice, and it was Jimmy. Don't get me wrong, if I hadn't sent it I could have walked away without him even knowing but I waited on him and we had a good chat, he was on holiday in Sydney and helping out at a hostel just up the road, it was great to meet him again. That was during the week and on the Saturday Susanne and I were in the mall to get Ronan Keating's autograph for Cheryl who was a huge Boyzone and Ronan fan. We were standing in the queue when who came along but Jimmy, he was getting his book for his sister's birthday. So, if I hadn't sent the money and I had walked away during the week, he would have still caught me, now back to Lawrence and Margaret.

I borrowed Adam from the works utility van to go to pick up some bits and pieces, it had no power steering and on turning the wheel I cracked my neck, and a shooting pain went right up my head. On Saturday the guests arrived, and we picked them up at the Manly Ferry. They were very disappointed initially at Manly Beach, they thought where the ferry came in that was it, we drove around the other side of the corso and there they saw the Manly Beach, impression changed.

We had been to a garage sale that morning and had bought a suite from a lovely Taiwanese family at the end of the street who were going back home. We paid four hundred dollars for it but I reckon it was a five thousand plus purchase for them, it was huge, one time when Cheryl and Emma stayed the four of us crashed out on the suite. It was in three pieces and very light so Lawrence and I carried it home and as we did so there was Susanne running towards us with the Olympic torch, someone in the area was a designated carrier and Susanne asked for a shot, you can take the girl out of Glasgow but not Glasgow out of the girl. It was a great suite and will turn up again in this book. All afternoon Lawrence and I were in the pool playing headers, they stayed the night and left later in the day as they were staying with Margaret's Uncle and Aunt who were driving them crazy taking them to old people's places, they really wanted to stay with us but not up for saying to Margaret's family.

Monday lunchtime I am walking to the Mall to get lunch when pains start shooting up my neck and head, I go back to the car and head to the doctors in Manly, the receptionist shouts the doctor out right away and the doctor orders me to sit down I say I prefer to stand and she shouts if you don't sit down you will fall down. My blood pressure was through the roof, and she piled tablets and an injection into me. The ambulance took me the short distance to Manly hospital where I was immediately put in a dark cupboard. I was given lots of pills and a few injections to try and stabilise my blood pressure and after a while the pain started to ease off. The first thoughts of the doctors in the hospital were that I could have had an aneurism therefore they ordered a lumbar puncture to be performed. This is a very painful thing and luckily Susanne was there to hold my hand, but the ironic thing was that the procedure was being done by a trainee called Dr Motherwell who came from Motherwell in Scotland, I thought he was saying that to take the pain out of the equation but sorry doctor it didn't. No aneurysm which was good, and it turned out that I had destroyed all the muscles in my neck and the tissue was all torn hence the blood getting through so quickly. I was in the hospital for three days and then physio for a few weeks, now and again I get some twinges in my neck and head, but it still feels good.

As we were building the furniture Susanne invited me for a coffee in Manly one afternoon. We had the coffee just across from this Art Studio and it was suggested we should take a pop in, coffee $6 painting $600 a pretty dear coffee. The painting I must admit is excellent, it is of the Oceanids statue at Shelley Beach just next to Manly, funny in that I call Cheryl Shelley. Susanne had been working in the Medical Centre at the Mall but found a new job at Freedom Furniture where she met a good few new people and we had some good parties with them, Helen a lady from Paisley in Scotland had joined the company also and it turned out she stayed in the same complex as us when we moved to Fairlight. The boss though was an arse on holidays, Susanne wanted to go back to Scotland for a few weeks for some events that were coming up, but he only ever wanted you to take a week which suited him and not many more people. I was also having issues with Kerry. He was buying things like three MP3 players which were for his kids with the company money and replacing new computers with newer ones and they were all disappearing, I even held the door open for him on one occasion. Susanne was getting worried that I might lose it with him and get kicked out of the country. It was also the time for me to look at applying for permanent residency and when I left the UK the company told me they would pay all fees, Kerry was not having it, basically he was paid a bonus on the profit of the company, and he wasn't giving any of his money away.

I was going on a trip to Melbourne, Adelaide and Perth which would take me away for a couple of weeks. The first weekend I was in Adelaide and Susanne had been having problems that week with a mouse and noises coming from the fireplace. She wanted me to come home and cancel the rest of the trip, I told her I couldn't as it was booked by the company. She got a specialist out and he put his hand in the fireplace and said oh there is something in there, wow what a specialist he was, turns out it was a possum that was having babies, the mouse if I remember right left of its own accord.

We used to go into a pub called Cheers in Sydney City Centre to watch Rangers and Celtic games. Upstairs was the Rangers end and downstairs the Celtic end, we are one of each. I would go downstairs with her so that she was not on her own and one match in particular Celtic took the lead just before half-time and that is the way it finished. The pub emptied quickly, and I noticed Joe Miller the ex-Aberdeen and Celtic winger. We went over to talk to him, and he was very welcoming. We had a chat and I told him I was the token Rangers supporter here and he said probably as his mate left at half-time with the score at 1-0. He had come over to play with a team called Parramatta Power and he had stayed on hoping to get into coaching.

A few weeks later Susanne and I were going to put Lottery tickets on and walked along the beach at Manly. We went to go up the stairs and I recognised a guy standing at the top of the stairs staring out to sea. Hello Ian, I said and startled him, he responded oh hi how you are doing. Ian Ferguson had arrived on the Northern Beaches to play for Northern Spirit who at that time were owned by Rangers. It was his first day here and we chatted for a while and I suggested he should catch up with Joe, turned out he had already done so and was meeting him later in the week.

For the Millennium we went to my cousin Sarah's (Sadie in Scotland) in Capalaba where my uncle Daniel (Dad's brother) and his wife Jean were. They were there on holiday which Daniel loved as it was full on party time. It was a great weekend and so good to catch up with family and while I had been to Sadies a few times since I came to Australia it was an incident back in Scotland many years before that was a strange one. I went to Uncle Daniels place for New Year and Sadie and her then husband Iain were there, it was the first time I had seen her for many years, she used to love coming to our house in Alderman Road with her dad and she was so spoiled by my mum. Second week January I am back at work and going along M8 motorway in the back of the bosses car with legs up on the seat looking back the way, see this car behind us and I start waving, all of a sudden Sadie realises it is me, she is in the car behind us, not seen her for years and see her twice in the space of a few days.

Our second New Year we went to Sydney Harbour along with the other couple of people that were there, they reckon around quarter of a million all around the harbour and stood next to a guy who was travelling and stayed just outside Glasgow, turns out I played pool against his brother for years. Great night but nightmare getting to and from toilets, took around 40 minutes to do this but worth it.

Our third year was spent on a boat under the harbour bridge with Cheryl and her friend Emma and Stevie Donald and his wife Margaret who came over from Perth, this was the first time I had seen Stevie since he emigrated although had spoken to him a few times on the phone after scouring phonebooks and eventually finding him. I must say I spoke with and left messages with around a dozen Donald's around Australia who were all Scottish. Great night out until Margaret had to take off her high heels and her feet were destroyed is probably the best word I could use.

Susanne's mum and Brother Eddie came out to visit us and we had a great time with them, the pool was a big plus and one of the highlights was the Melbourne Cup Day at the Ivanhoe hotel, they couldn't believe how big this was and we have a picture of Eddie swinging on a tree after he won $10. Susanne went home with them and didn't come back for five months, I think she was considering her future and missing her mum so for that time I took in a lodger Robert, a software developer who had split from his wife, and was going to help with the rent. He was okay but smoked a lot and I kept telling him to get outside, sometimes I would come home and smell it right away and a couple of times I caught him sitting on the settee watching TV smoking. On a Saturday I would come back from Golf and go for a nap before going out, but he was bringing his kids over now and they were in the pool all day screaming, he was getting on my nerves. It was Robert who woke me the night that 9/11 was happening telling me they were crashing planes into buildings, we sat up the whole night watching it. Susanne came back and we spent another few months at the house with the pool.

Susanne persuaded me to join in a St Patricks Day parade through Sydney organised through her work colleagues. It was being led by the Manly Warringah Pipe Band and I reluctantly joined in. After the parade we were in the pub and got talking to a band member who played the bagpipes. I asked if he had Scottish heritage and he said not that he knew off and next question why the bagpipes, he told me he stayed on the Northern Beaches at Double Bay and his neighbour put in plans for an extension which was approved however it was not adhered to and he lost some of his view across the bay so he decided he would make their lives hell. He took up the pipes and after a few months he had to move as all the other neighbours fell out with him!!! Out of that parade and stalls we bought a hideous looking large Shamrock with costume jewellery which Susanne wanted to take back to her mum in Glasgow, what a nightmare trying to explain it at Changi Airport.

We were paying a high rent for the house, and we decided to downsize as we were going back to Scotland again for a three-week holiday and didn't fancy paying money for nothing. We found a small flat in Balgowlah this time it was about a kilometre from the last place and a different suburb again. It was pokey after having the house and we struggled, and we fought with the owners for various reasons, not least the five hours it would take to do a small chicken in the oven because of all the seals needing replaced, it was a short stay.

We moved again four hundred metres to another suburb in Fairlight just across from Manly Golf Club and this was more like us big and spacious with a car parking space however I could not get the use of it as every time I went to park in it someone was in it. One night I decided to park in front of it to see what happened. Next morning the door gets chapped and when I open it there is this giant of a man who I had noticed had a gym in his garage and he used to do pull ups on his balcony, a lot of pull ups too. He tells me I have blocked his wife's car in and she had to go to work, I told him she shouldn't be parking there, he says they thought the flat was still unoccupied and he agreed. Turns out he was from Drumchapel in Glasgow, and he proceeded to tell me that he used to go to the gym just up the road from him which I could see easily. He wasn't telling any lies, so I told him that wasn't far from my shooting club!!! (Never went to a shooting club but thought it sounded good in the conversation). Cheryl and her friend Emma came to see us at this house for three months. I went to the airport dressed as Santa and lo and behold in the main concourse there was a Santa seat. Susanne met the girls and told them I had trouble parking and would get them outside. They walked past the seat I jumped up and frightened the life out of them with all the rest of the people in the airport in stitches.

They discovered if they went to the Steyne pub early enough before the bouncers came on, they could stay there all night. So, they would leave about 5.00pm and get sausage and mash for dinner then stay out until the early hours. I had mentioned to them that they must see the dawn breaking over Manly beach and how spectacular it was. One morning Susanne and I got up for work and mentioned that we never heard the kids coming in, around about seven thirty the door opens and there is Cheryl and Emma I asked where they had been and they said watching the sunrise at Manly beach, I said I meant get up early in the morning and see it not stay out all night, they were young and there is no argument for that.

I was well into the golf club now and the boys were taking a trip to Melbourne to play two great courses, The Victorian and Kingston Heath and take in the Rugby World Cup last eight matches between South Africa and New Zealand on the Saturday night and France and Ireland on the Sunday. We landed at lunchtime in Melbourne and went straight to the hotel to dump the bags and golf clubs then we headed out.

We went to a few different pubs but ended up in a huge one which was nearly full, there was a big English contingent in there and they started singing Swing Low Sweet Chariot which upset a good few of the locals, they were very good though and I thought it needed a response so in my best singing voice I leapt into you can stick your fucking chariots up your arse, you can stick your fucking chariots up your arse, you can stick your fucking chariots, stick your fucking chariots, stick your fucking chariots up your arse to which the whole pub had joined in minus the English among us but they did see the funny side of it. On the tram to the ground Adam couldn't stop singing it and again the whole tram was joining in.

New Zealand won the game on Saturday night easily and we left the stadium to go and sample the nightlife in Melbourne. We had been to a few pubs and clubs, and we decided that it was time to go as we're going to play golf tomorrow, where's Johnny, no sign of him. We worked on the principle that he had just done the casual fade and left; we looked around for him but decided it was time to go back to the hotel. It turns out he had come out of the pub for a smoke and went back into the wrong one. Also turns out he was trying to get into the building next door to the hotel with his swipe card until three Irish guys helped him out.

We went to The Victoria Golf Club and from memory it looked great but really, I do not remember playing it. I don't think the others were much better, but they didn't admit it. We went back to the hotel and had a nap before heading out for the France and Ireland game on Sunday night. France won easily which was a shame as the banter and patter from the Irish crowd was brilliant. On the way back I provided the guys with another gem which all the Irish guys bought into. If I had the wings of a sparrow and I had the arse of a crow I'd fly over France tomorrow and shite on the bastards below. Well Adam took to this and by the end of the night he was singing it Pavarotti style at the top of his voice, we didn't stay out late that night as Kingston Heath was earlier in the morning, what a golf course though, thoroughly enjoyed it and played well, Johnny won of course. I stayed in Melbourne for work and the boys headed back to Sydney.

Kingston Heath Golf Club, James, Johnny and Adam

I stupidly took part in a Decathlon at the club not long after joining as one of the guys had to pull out at the last minute. I agreed to keep the numbers to sixteen and this luxury cost me $100.00 for entry. It was on a Friday at 6.00am and started off with nine holes of golf, I came 3rd. Next was the five kilometre run or for me walk, then on to the two hundred metre swim, break. Next was basketball hoops, ten pin bowling then back to club for 100m sprint which I surprised two people by beating them, Geoff was the club pro and a bit older and one of the other guys pulled a hamstring. I am missing one here but cannot for the life of me remember what. Then indoors to my arena, beaten semis at Table Tennis, won the pool and the darts and finished tenth, not bad for someone who hadn't had any practice.

I went to play as usual on the Saturday and never had any problems where some of the younger guys were saying they had some aches and pains. Sunday morning and the rest of the week our neighbours thought Susanne and I had the best sex life ever as every time I moved I was in agony and squealing with pain.

I became captain of the club and so was on the board of directors, we had lost $40,000 the previous year, we worked hard to turn this around which we did by selling two licences for fruit machines on the premises which nobody played and these went for $11,000 each. The equipment we had was very old and repairs alone were costing us $2,000 per month so we scrapped the lot and rented brand new equipment at a cost of $1,500 per month. We had our first revolt from the older members about this saying it wasn't the way to use the money and believe it or not a lot of them were accountants! The next revolt was directly against a decision I pushed through the board. We had the senior members who all played at various times of the day on a Wednesday but left right after golf and not using any of the facilities. I was approached by a guy I knew who worked for the Master Builders Association and they wanted to hire the club and have lunch along with 9 holes of golf but the only day they could do it was a Wednesday. So rather than call a meeting of the members I proposed to the board we move the Wednesday competition and make $10,000. Well the uproar was brilliant and I thoroughly enjoyed it but it did go ahead and we did get $10,000 so decision justified. My success at the club was winning the club foursomes championship with Steven Painter and winning a monthly medal which is the toughest club tournament to win. James and I played in a tournament at a club called Roseville in the North of the Northern Beaches and was attended by Captains and Board members from throughout New South Wales, we won it and it was the first time Balgowlah had won it since the 1920's.

We got pretty close to Helen and Tony; she was married to a Scottish sailor, and they had split up a good few year earlier. Tony was a great big guy who got brought up with his two brothers on the banks of the

Swan River in Perth, he sounded like a modern-day Tom Sawyer with his stories. Sadly, in January of the following year Tony passed away, he was on his tea break at his work and reading his paper and one of his mates shouted at him to get back to work and he was dead. We went to see him in his coffin just before the service. He was dressed in his budgie smugglers (Speedo swimming trunks), his headrest for reading at the beach, a can of VB beer, and suntan oil. Helen said her goodbyes, Susanne said her goodbyes and I leaned in to tell him what a great guy he was and how I would miss him but moving away I didn't lift my arms high enough and they caught on the coffin which started swivelling. Helen and Susanne raced over to help, and we averted the big guy lying on the floor in his speedos as the congregation came in. PHEW. Helen had a real strange character about her, as we say in Scotland she could start a fight in an empty house. We took her to the club one night for a quiz night and she ended up embarrassing us in front of all the members, we persevered because she was Scottish and a neighbour. She appears later in the book and watch out for that one.

This was a bad time for all of us as the following month Adam and Deb lost their first baby Riley to Sudden Infant Death Syndrome on his first day at kindergarten. Deb went to pick him up around four and saw the ambulance outside, so sad, he was just six months old. That meant we had two funerals in the space of a few weeks, Tony aged sixty-two and Riley just six months. I had never been to a baby's funeral before, and I hope I never go to another one.

In the club we looked at doing something for the SIDS and Kids Foundation and later in the year we organised a golf day at Balgowlah which raised $50,000 dollars and the following year we did the same and raised the same amount of money for the same Foundation. Kris Barkway the pro at the time also did a 24-hour golf challenge which he completed but with a bit of pain, cannot remember the total Kris raised but what a great effort.

Sids Day - Deb, Jo, Tracey and Liz, Pete, BJ, Johnny, Me and Kris finishing his 24 hour golf challenge

The Fairlight kindergarten had another tragedy not long after Riley's passing when an elderly driver came down the hill opposite the Kindy and ploughed straight into it, two kids were very seriously injured and badly burned. One of the girls was called Sophie Delezio and she had horrific injuries and was lucky to survive however she was very badly disabled, Sophie is mentioned again later.

It was around this time that we lost Susanne's father to pancreatic cancer, I was in Canberra when she phoned and I made a dash back to Sydney and on flight next day to Glasgow. My brother James was next, he had been unwell for a number of years but he was the most unconcious comedian I have ever known.

I reported Kerry to the bosses at HK Wentworth in the UK and with the help of Carmel in the office we produced lots of documentation including the company paying for his haircuts every week and when I told them about the car and the permanent residency situation they were seething. A few weeks later they came out to Australia and sacked him and made me general manager. Turns out he had also given them a false age; he was two years older than he said he was.

One of my first tasks was to go to our New Zealand site and spend some time with Eddie the HK Wentworth rep who only sold the AF brand because he feared the others. His ex-wife Leanne was in the office running that side. He drove a fancy supped up Ford XR 6 for his company car and we went on a trip around his customers. We got to the Airport as we were going to the South Island, he put his car in valet parking, and all right Eddie says the guy. We got to the Motel, all right Eddie and this went on wherever we went, he had been doing it for a good few years so maybe I was reading something into it that wasn't there.

We set out to see customers the next day and the round trip took us four days and three nights away in nice motels, not the most cost effective. The highlight for me was when we got to Invercargill to see one customer who Eddie had been going to see for years. I asked him what their monthly spend was and he says $25 per month. We had driven three hours to get there, stayed overnight, had a meal and this customer was spending that amount. I asked Eddie how often he did this, and he says every month!!! We had spent the customers' annual spend that day and maybe even a bit more and he didn't get what the problem was. Invercargill is one of the most southerly and Westerly points of New Zealand. Leanne used to get the orders via email, check them and send them on to the 3rd party company we used to keep stock and deliver the products. The office was a great big one with all the best gear, new printer, new phone system and fancy paintings on the wall. We had a cleaner who came in most days, and I thought they were taking the piss.

On the flight back from Auckland I prepared a report for the senior management which recommended we close the New Zealand Office and make the two of them redundant. Mark and Rob came out for a few days, one of which would be an overnight stay in Auckland, this was to be done on their second day coming from the UK. I told Eddie that we were coming across and that Mark and Rob would only be staying overnight and leaving early next morning. Eddie picked us up at the airport and took us to Eden Park to show us the stadium then on to the office, it was approximately 4.00pm, they went around the office, and spoke with both Eddie and Leanne to get a handle on how the company worked in New Zealand. Eddie then dropped us off at 6.00pm at the three hundred dollars a night each hotel saying he would pick us up for dinner at 6.30pm. He had booked a restaurant on one of the islands and the ferry was at 7.00pm which took about 20-30 minutes to get there. Even before we got there the guys were shattered, I asked Eddie what time the ferry was booked for back and he said 11.00pm. I told him that would not be happening and to look at the guys. The five of us had dinner and the bill came to nearly $200 and we headed back on the 9.00pm ferry and walked the short distance to the hotel. Rob suggested a night cap and we went into the bar, ordered a few Drambuie, and then came the instruction, shut it down. The guys left the next morning early having spent just six hours in their $300 a night hotel. I moved out the next day too and went into my usual $55 a night motel.

TERRY DUFF (WEE GLASGOW GUY)

I stayed the weekend in New Zealand and was in a bar watching the rugby league international with Australia on the TV when I got one of the best laughs of my life. There was a couple sitting at the bar in front of me and Australia had a breakaway, and the girl starts shouting in her Kiwi accent "Tickle him" "Tickle him" well the vision will live with me forever as a big brawny Kiwi is running alongside a big brawny Aussie tickling the life out of him.

On another visit to New Zealand, I was in the hotel and on TV there was a fundraising night run by the All-Blacks Rugby team, one of the guests was the famous boxer Joe Frazier who sang Mustang Sally, very badly I must add. Next day at the airport waiting to go through security an American guy tapped me on the shoulder and said watch this, this is funny. It was Joe taking off all his jewellery, six rings, four bracelets, ten chains and he was holding up the queue, guy keeps saying to keep watching and eventually he goes through the scanner beep, beep, beep, turns out he has two metal plates in his shoulders, the guy was his manager, and he says the same rigmarole happens at every airport. I got a cracking picture taken with Joe but when I left the employment of HK Wentworth it was on their phone, bugger.

By now I was looking after Australia, New Zealand, and some customers in Japan as well as Hakko the soldering equipment supplier. I was also going back to the UK four times a year, January, April, July, and

October for senior management meetings. I used to leave Sydney Thursday and arrive in Glasgow Friday lunchtime, spend the weekend with family and friends. I would then get the early morning flight down to East Midlands on the Monday morning and straight into meetings, this is when the jet lag started to kick in. We stayed in an old farmhouse not far from the office in Swadlincote, every night one of the directors John would make meat and two veg, one night beef, one night lamb etc. and on the Monday, I would have dinner, a couple of glasses of red wine and bed by eight o'clock. Each night after that I gained an extra hour of staying up, Thursday we normally had a full team get together and stayed up until around 11.00pm then bed. We finished around 3.00pm on Friday and I would either get a lift or taxi back to Heathrow for the 10.00pm flight back to Sydney. With the time difference I would not get back there until Sunday morning and going that way the jet lag is a hundred times worse as you are losing the hours and the short time I was away made it worse. I would try to stay awake, but it was impossible and generally on the Monday morning I was in the office at 2.00am, security would call when I went in, and they would say that you back home from the UK Terry.

I was approached by a South African gentleman by the name of Alasdair who had moved to Sydney around the same time as myself, he wanted to become a distributor for our company as this was what he had done in his home country. He lived in Newcastle three hours north of Sydney and would travel down most days of the week to visit customers which I found strange as it made for long days. Turns out he had a counterpart Paul in Ballarat three hours west of Melbourne and he done the same. It took a while but I discovered they were part of the religious cult known as Exclusive or Closed Brethren who only broke bread with and generally done business with their own kind, things like printing and accounting would all be kept within the group. No TV or even computers at that time were used by the group. They are a Christian Evangelical group they did not pay the same taxes as others and they used to build their communities in areas away from main cities. On a trip to see a customer in Tamworth five hours north of Sydney who were involved in the rainwater industry I met David also from South Africa, he asked me when I had arrived in Australia and told him it was May 1999, he said he had come the same month and I just blurted out do you know Alasdair and Paul and he told me Alasdair was his old business partner in Cape Town and Paul was his brother in law. In 2019 I went on a joint visit with a supplier to a company in South Queensferry near Edinburgh and as soon as he stepped out of his car I knew he was Brethren, I didn't reveal anything that I knew about them, however on the phone a while later to Darryl in the office for this supplier based in Irvine he told me he was going to Australia, I asked if he was going to Newcastle and he said yes and I straight out asked him if he knew Alasdair and he told me that he was his father in law, weird or what. They do not vote but managed to give then Premier John Howard an $8 million dollar donation.

I came back to Scotland to surprise Cheryl for her 18th birthday, I had told her I was going to be in New Zealand for work but had booked a round the world flight path to keep costs down believe it or not. I booked via Qantas and British Midland from Heathrow to Glasgow. Although booked via Qantas the planes were British Airways to London and there was a 3 hour delay in Sydney which meant I missed my connecting flight. I was also a British Midland Silver member and went to their desk, it was around 9.00am and they told me they could get me on a flight at 11.30am but they only had Business Class available, this would be £183, I told them to stick it and went to British Airways the only other company to fly this route and they quoted me £184 and not available until 1.00pm. Tail between legs back to BM where I paid the money and confirmed I could go into the Business lounge. It was empty and I went around opening every packet of sandwiches, crisps, chocolate and cans of juice. While downing a few glasses of wine. On the plane I ordered champagne and more food which I did not touch but opened.

Anyway back to Cheryl, she was gobsmacked when I turned up and we got to spend a good bit of time for the week I was there. I travelled light just having a hold all with me which didn't have a padlock on it. I flew BM to Heathrow and then British Airways to New York and then on to Los Angeles where we had to take our bags and check in again for the flight to Sydney. It was Qantas staff and I was second in the queue but the guy at our line was new and had to keep asking for assistance while the lady on the other side was processing people through. Eventually he got to me and I gave him my bag and he threw it on to a trolley which I had heard the other lady was for Asia, I pointed this out to him and he told me it would be sorted out downstairs. I arrived in Sydney during a baggage handlers strike and waited, eventually a guy came up the travelator, he was one of the managers doing the unloading and he said he would go down and double check for my bag, I told him not to bother as my bag would be in Asia. He gave me the claim form if it didn't turn up or was damaged and a few days later the bag turned up with various country stickers on it. Inside missing was all the new stuff that I was bringing back for Susanne from the family and a couple of things of mine. I filled in the form and a few weeks later get a cheque for $240 and a letter, the money was for 20 kilos at $12 per kilo. I told Susanne I was not pleased a) with the money as there was a lot of gifts there and b) The last part of the letter says Qantas does not accept any responsibility or liability for the loss or damage. Right now for one of my famous letters, told them the story of my trip with BA and BM to Los Angeles, and it wasn't until you bastards at Qantas got your hands on it that the problem started. Two weeks later a cheque and a letter arrives for $865 and the comment at the bottom that Qantas does not accept any responsibility or liability for the loss or damage, Susanne looked at me with those don't you dare eyes so the letters were finished to Qantas.

On my trip one year in April I was checking in at Heathrow and I asked the lady checking me in if she had long to go before she finished and she told me I was her last one and that the next day she was off to Mauritius for her daughter's wedding, I thanked her and told her to have a great time. In July that year I had foolishly taken my golf clubs and got them checked in no problem at Sydney as I was a Platinum Qantas Club Member. We got to Glasgow on the Thursday night around 7.00pm which had been the first day of the British Open Golf. The clubs never made the connecting flight and we were in a queue of people from various parts of the world whose luggage had not made it to Glasgow. I got to the front and the girl asked me what it was that was missing and I told her it was my golf clubs and she said they would be delivered tomorrow, I told her that tomorrow was not good enough as I was playing in the British Open next day, the giggles and laughs from the queue mostly Americans here for the golf made it a worthwhile comment and the clubs duly turned up around 10.00pm that night.

We were going to celebrate Susanne's fortieth and had through the family arranged a surprise party or it was nearly a surprise. We had met a couple of Irish sisters who were travelling and they became friends of our group, Johnny the greenkeeper was seeing Aisling. They actually stayed next door to people who were customers of RD Taylors in Limerick. The girls had done their travelling and were now back in Ireland but we had arranged for them to be in Glasgow, we had a few people around in the afternoon and Johnny was just leaving when he says to Susanne, you must be looking forward to seeing the girls at your party, another DOH!!!! Thanks Johnny.

On the way back from that trip we were due on the 11.00am to Heathrow and then changing terminals to fly to Sydney. We were both hung over and when we got to the British Airways check in desk I was told that there would be a £330 charge to get the clubs back to Sydney, I explained that I was a Qantas Platinum member and that it was reciprocal with BA and she said she would check with her superior. She came back and said they would do it for £300 or I could put them on the plane to Heathrow for nothing and collect them there. I opted for the latter and was raging and when we got to Heathrow it took an eternity for them to come through, we were cutting it fine as we had to get from Terminal one to Terminal four via train. We eventually get to check in which we can do at the business desk although we were flying economy. It was a small queue and when we got to the desk there was someone training and the lady beside her was the same one who had dealt with me in April. I asked how her daughter's wedding had went in Mauritius and she was gobsmacked and asked how I knew and I told her I was the last person she had checked in before finishing for holiday. She told me that this had nothing to do with my comments to her but we had been upgraded to Business Class, first time ever. We got on the plane and they brought us champagne, I took some and promptly went straight to the toilet and threw up. I never touched a drop or had anything to eat the whole journey, Susanne gave it a bit of a try but not great for first time. We have had the pleasure of flying Business Class on a number of occasions with Emirates but generally using up the points I had accumulated with all the flying I was doing.

On another occasion I had arrived back in Glasgow for a holiday on the Friday and Bud suggested we go to watch the Scottish Open Golf at Loch Lomond, we were standing on the boat and Ernie Els was marking his ball on the green and a freelance photographer took a picture of that with Bud, Mark and I in the background, it appeared on the back page of the Sunday Mail. It was an eventful day as we went from the Golf to the pub in Luss further up the loch. There was a young couple in there and the boys told me the guy was golfer Ian Poulter, he had loads of fancy gear on and I went over and introduced myself saying I was visiting from Australia, the guy just stared straight through me and I turned to see Mark, Bud, Pammy and Lynn all in hysterics. We had a few that day and on getting back to the jetty we had to get on the dinghy to get ashore, I threw my phone and wallet to the guys already on the jetty and proceeded to fall off the dinghy straight into Loch Lomond.

Bud and I at golf, Ernie Els putting with Me, Mark and Bud on boat and the Loch Lomond Dip

I also had a few trips to Japan which were amazing. I read up on doing business in Japan and the book told me the first thing you will be asked is what food you do not like and sure as anything when Morioka from Hakko picked me up at the airport that was the question, I said raw fish and basically anything fishy. My first meal in Osaka where Hakko were based was spaghetti bolognese, I had pancake's the next day for lunch which were interesting as they basically put anything you want on a pancake. Second trip was for a Trade show in Tokyo. I went to Hakko Osaka first and then we got the Shinkansen bullet train to Tokyo. What an experience that was, three hundred and fifty kilometres an hour and I got the best photos of Mount Fuji from the train.

In Tokyo the Hakko teams had a challenge to provide the entertainment. The first night was a sampan trip around Tokyo harbour and it was amazing and at the dinner I decided to get adventurous in the eating stakes. Morioka had ordered me chicken but when all the seafood came out, I just had to try as it was so colourful, I am now a big sushi and sashimi fan.

Night two was a banquet and again the seafood was spectacular and again I delved right in, and the entertainment was the group challenging each other to tell jokes which wasn't great for all the people who were there from all over the world but hey.

Night three saw the Sales team effort and this was one of the most fantastic things I have ever seen.

We had dinner and then we went to the bowling alley, and everyone was thinking bowling, how boring but we went past the bowling alley and into a room at the back where there was Karaoke, not any Karaoke but magic Karaoke. It started with the president of Hakko, a 42-year-old woman who had just taken over from her father, cannot remember what she sang but wow, turns out she was a trained opera singer. A few great singers followed and the guy I was with Steve got up to go to the toilet and as he walked out the door the call went up for Ando, the place erupted. It turns out Ando is famous for this song and as he burst into the Copacabana there were people on the seats and on the tables it was mental. Ando finished to a rapturous applause and Steve walked back in, I told him you would never believe what just happened here and it was truly amazing. The night went on and fizzled out when the two polish distributors sang a song, not karaoke but about Lech Walesa and the Polish revolution or something like that.

The sales teams went on to a couple of clubs and had a good night and it was crazy but the one thing I noticed the next day was that no one discussed the night before at all as if nothing had happened.

Michikazu Gyobo became our new rep, and he visited Sydney a couple of times, what a lovely man but as blind as a bat, he was young maybe 23-24 and I asked how his eyesight got so bad for one so young. He explained that lots of young Japanese people wear

MEET YRRET FFUD

My Kimono, Ando and the Copacabana, Sampan in
Tokyo Harbour and Mt Fuji from bullet train

glasses and contact lenses and he reckoned and not sure how true this is but because they live in big cities with large populations, they don't get to see many colours like the grass and other things, the cities are full of grey buildings and their eyesight gets used to seeing the same colours. Mich if you were taking the piss, you have won this one. It is a very common thing that Japanese people are not very good with the letter R, they generally pronounce as L. It was not meant but I told Mich that I was taking him to a famous meat restaurant called

Ribs and Rumps. He spent the whole day when in the car trying to say it correctly and I don't think I have laughed so much in one day. He would say it soft and then get to shouting it but honestly he never mastered it and that night we had dinner at Libs and Lumps.

One visit Michikazu came with Yoji Hayase who was born in Brisbane, it was for a trade show we were doing at Darling Harbour. They were booked on the 10.00am flight back to Osaka on Sunday and I had taken them for dinner and into the Steyne pub in Manly which was open until 4.00am, they were staying at Darling Harbour. I was going home around 1.00am as I had to play golf the next day, I suggested I get them a taxi, but they were having none of it, sleep on the plane I was told. Before I left, I went up and started dancing with a lovely blonde girl and I asked her if my friends could join in and that they were Japanese, she said no problem she was studying Japanese, what are the chances. I left the guys to it, and I believe they just made the flight and no more.

On another visit to the beautiful Darling Harbour we were sitting having lunch, Susanne and I, Cheryl and Emma when Susanne asked if we wanted to turn around and there walking into the restaurant was Mr Rangers Ally McCoist, funny it was the only Celtic supporter in the group who spotted him. We went to talk to him and was very welcoming, he was on a break from Question of Sport and from memory he had just been playing five asides. I had to tell him about an evening visit to Ibrox which started off with us being in the queue to get in to the main stand and a couple of guys were walking to the front and I told the guys that one of them was Paddy Crerand (Celtic and Manchester United legend) I was rebuffed with don't be stupid what would he be doing at a Rangers game. Next minute from the front of the queue came the holler, hey Crerand get yourself to fuck. Duff wins again. It was a European game in November and it was freezing, we were in the back row and after about ten minutes we were down to t shirts as the atmosphere was electric. It was against Dynamo Kiev and the first goal the goalkeeper went to throw the ball out and it hit his defenders back and McCoist toe poked it to Mark Falco to score the opener. Rangers second goal was a classic by all standards, a great cross from Francis, headed across the box and there was super Ally to head into the net, he looked to head the ball in to the right hand side of the goal which is where the goalkeeper was heading but it came off the side of his head into the left side of the goal, genius Mr McCoist. We went on to win the tie and bought two of the opposing team who performed very well for Rangers.

We had moved again and this time we bought a place in Manly Vale, another suburb five hundred metres from the house in Fairlight. Six moves, six different suburbs and we were still in a two-mile radius from our starting point. This was a two-bedroom apartment with a wraparound balcony which we loved. It had a spa bath which was used every Friday with Sushi Sashimi platters for dinner and wine in the Spa. The suite was still with us and decided to get it recovered at a cost of $2,000 and it was green to match décor in the new flat. This was the only place apart from the house we bought it in that it actually fitted in.

I had been asking Ron the Managing Director about my salary and bonus as well as new equipment for the warehouse. We were storing class six chemicals in normal shelving without any special flammable cabinets which was really worrying me as the temperatures in Sydney can get very high, throw in a type of glass roof and panic stations. I also wanted my salary reviewed for all the extra work I was doing but it kept getting put off until next visit. The last time I went I was organising the three days that we were having a big get together of all the employees. When I got there nothing was set up and I had to do this in the first instance, then first morning the main man Gerald Kingsbury comes in an hour late and disrupts the whole session saying good morning to everyone in person. Second day same scenario and this was really getting on my nerves, this and the constant putting back of discussions with Ron. Last day of the conference was Thursday and Gerald came in late again and at this point I handed Ron a piece of paper about changing company culture with my resignation on the back. I went back to my room in the farmhouse and was changing my flight when Gerald came in and I think he was going to comfort me or ask me to think again but he just wanted back some papers he had given me, thanks Gerald. After eleven and a half years I left HK Wentworth for good. I flew out that Thursday night and back home to Sydney Saturday morning. I had told Ron that I had a week off and that I was going to play golf and he said he would speak with me when I got back.

I went with a crowd of guys on Monday to the South Coast of New South Wales where we played five rounds, Kiama, Nowra where you tee off from a cave, Kangaroo Valley which was stunning, and we played that twice and Kembla Grange on the way back up. On the Monday night Carmel from the office phoned to say they had changed all the locks, and no discussions ever took place. On the way back on the Friday heading to Balgowlah we got stopped on the Wakehurst Parkway due to an accident which we thought must be a fatality with all the police and ambulances around. We phoned ahead and found out that a child in a pushchair had been hit with a car on a pedestrian crossing. Oh my god it turned out to be the same little girl who had been injured so badly in the kindergarten crash, Sophie Dolezio. How horrific for her and her family Sophie survived that crash too and the last time I looked on the internet she had grown into a beautiful young woman.

I enjoyed the three months garden leave, still had my company car and phone in case they needed to contact me for anything and played golf lots during this time. My handicap became the lowest it has ever been going from 11.4 down to 9.6 still couldn't make single figures with 9.6 being classed as 10 DOH.

On another golf outing we had three visitors with us who all had played or coached the Manly Rugby Union team, Paul, Doc, and Robbie were great guys and told us some great stories. The best was that they trained in the morning and then to Kelly's bar at the big Steyne pub, they would go home after a few hours in there and tell the wives that they had went to the gym in the afternoon and popped in for a couple. The wives were very suspicious of this, and the guys told this to the manager of the pub. Next week they go to training and then on to Kelly's which has now changed its name to Kelly's Gym what a genius thing to do and now the guys were not telling any lies.

Our Sydney crowd loved their music especially Ronnie who had sounds from all around the world. We had arranged to go and see The Eagles at the Dome next to the National sports stadium. We payed $150 each for the tickets but well worth it, they were on for three hours and every song they played you knew sensational. It was also the night when Joe Walsh admitted that he didn't drink alcohol anymore, says he got drunk once for forty years and then proceeded to play the opening bars of Life's Been Good To Me, amazing. Soon after we went to see Norah Jones at the Entertainment Centre and tickets were $125 and while it was a very good concert and enjoyable the pricing was not appropriate considering she was only on for one and a half hours.

Near the end of the garden leave it was time to start looking for a new job.

And now for something completely different, I had been selling specialty chemicals for most of my career and went for a role with a start-up company called Rain Harvesting who sold filtration systems for rainwater collection, after all Australia was in drought at this time. I got the job and took a forty percent wage drop to do so. My role was to build up the distribution of the products throughout Australia. The company was a start-up fronted by Sandy and his brother in law Gareth although the funding came from Sandy's father who had been head of a company called Herron Pharmaceuticals who were manufacturers of medicines and healthcare products. In 2000 they had to recall all products with paracetamol after a couple of people were hospitalised with strychnine poisoning, it was a blackmail attempt. The person was caught and charged but committed suicide while in custody.

I started well and picked up a few large chains to supply through, some had been buying bits and pieces as required but I managed to get more products added to the range. The biggest was Bunnings who had 150 stores throughout Australia. I also set up a training plan to support the range for all stores which proved very successful.

One of the companies I was successful with was a privately owned company called Hardware and general who had six facilities around Sydney, Peter McDonald looked after the sites, and he was based mainly at Brookvale, and we became very good friends. We had a meeting arranged at the Peakhurst site to do some training and it was bucketing down and the forecast was for storms. We were standing five yards from the front door having a cup of tea before the meeting when I heard the loudest noise I have ever heard, it was thunder right above us and next thing the lightning is bouncing just outside the door on the tarmac, wow what a fright. I had a few games of golf with Peter, and he was a 22 handicapper roughly as he was not a member of any club. When I moved away from the area, he joined Balgowlah Golf Club and one time when I was back down, I met up with him and he told me he had taken his clubs into the pro shop and asked them to sell them, he was going blind in his left eye and starting to struggle seeing the ball. The pro gave him some left-handed clubs to try, and he says he hit 1000 balls before he got on off the ground however he was now playing off 14 handicap, what a turnaround and what a lovely guy.

On another trip around the state of New South Wales I went to a few country towns including a stopover in Dubbo. I checked in and ordered a continental breakfast to be delivered to my room at around 7.30am. I got up around 6.30am and went in for a shower came out and made a cup of tea and sat out with laptop on the veranda anticipating breakfast coming however 7.30am came and went and nothing. I was looking to be on the road around 8.15am for my next customer visits and ended up packing up and checking out showing my displeasure at not having breakfast. The lady on the desk told me she had delivered it at around 7.00am and I told her she must have delivered to wrong door, she told me no it was definitely your room as she put it in the hatch. What? Every room seemingly has a hatch that they put food in to prevent animals stealing or being ruined by heat, we walked back and sure enough my breakfast was in the hatch, I thanked her and spent 15 minutes enjoying my breakfast.

The last night of this trip was to be spent in Bathurst and a morning meeting with a company called Clark Tanks however one thing you should never do is visit this town when the V8 Supercars motor racing is on. The weekend is taken up with petrol heads from all around the country and New Zealand and used to be and not sure still is a Holden versus Ford challenge although other cars were involved. It has a 12 hour endurance race and is held around the Mount Panorama racing circuit. I really struggled to get a room for the night and got lucky with what was probably the only room left in the town. Clark Tanks were next to the racing circuit and the customer I was seeing and I sat out in the sunshine having a meeting and listening to the roars of the practice rounds on the Friday morning. Well into the meeting we heard a real strange sound coming from the distance and watched as a plane crashed in to the mountain, not near the race track but then again not too far. It turns out it was an unlicensed tourist plane and the three occupants perished. I did get to go around the Bathurst track on a later visit but not at the speeds these guys were driving.

Bud, Margaret, Wee Bud, Martin and Susanne's mum came to see us in Manly Vale. Wee Bud is a beautiful kid who suffers from hydrocephalus and is hyperactive. We got back to the flat and we have two doors, one for each side of the balcony, he would go out one and come in the other now and again locking them. We shouted at him for breakfast, and he was trying to come in the locked door, strong bugger he is pulls the door frame away from the wall.

We had booked them into an apartment overlooking the middle surf club in Manly beach and we had a little party one Saturday night where a couple of Bud's friends from the Western Suburbs came along too. I don't think it was overly loud but the German couple on the next balcony did think so and I must say I was not overly impressed by the comments from our side. The place we rented the apartment from was downstairs from the flat and just on the corner where I had first stayed, handy if anything goes wrong.

Good Friday and we went across to the beach with the drink and the food for the day, Bud, Martin, and I were in the water throwing the ball around, it was rough, and we were not between the flags which is a big no. Suddenly, the ball starts to go out the way, Bud turns to get it, he is a good swimmer, but the ocean seems to have caught him out a bit and I swim out to help him. We get out of the water and sit down for some more socialising. Five minutes later I see Bud back in the water wandering around, I go to ask him what he is doing, and he says nothing, just a wee paddle. I do not buy this one, what are you doing? I am looking for the house keys, whit yeah, they must have fallen out of my pocket, and I told him they were probably halfway to Tasmania by now. No problem, the rental place is downstairs, problem, Good Friday everything is closed. Solution bearing in mind they are three floors up, chap German couple's door, climb over balcony and in as the veranda door is open. Mission accomplished with a degree of heart in mouth and tail between legs with the German couple.

Next visitor was James McCormack a good friend of ours and a right character, not surprised as his whole male side of the family were bonkers. James had been to visit family in Adelaide and was heading to Sydney for a week then on to see the rest of Australia. The first weekend he was there we took him to the Harbord Diggers Club which was a large Retired Services League building, while Britain has sadly done very poorly with veterans these places were set up to support their veterans. They still play the last post at six pm every night ending with the Lest We Forget phrase. We had bought quite a few raffle tickets as they had around twenty prizes and drawn in the afternoon. Around five hundred people in the place and first draw we win a meat tray, around $30 worth and perfect for the BBQ, a few draws later then a fish tray, then another meat tray, then the TV and finally another meat tray. It was very embarrassing and the looks we got were amazing. Sadly James passed away not long after his visit to Australia.

We went away for a long weekend to Hamilton Island which is in the Whitsunday's and home to the barrier reef. We went on a couple of tours including snorkelling in the barrier reef itself which is an amazing place. One night we left the veranda door slightly ajar and went to bed, next thing we hear is the clatter of dishes and we jump up to see the large white parrot slamming back into the door trying to escape, we had left some food scraps on the table and turns out they are real scavengers and take every opportunity to get food.

MEET YRRET FFUD

Sus and I reef ready, floating after dives and that bloody parrot

Another time Susanne's mum was coming to stay, Susanne's cousin Peter was already with us and he was a nightmare, he slept all day and was up all-night watching TV. We told him he needed to leave as Susanne's mum was coming but he had such a good number he kept putting it off. We eventually got him out the day before mum arrived and even got him a place to stay with Helen which didn't last long. This made us very wary about taking in people from then on in. Cue Claire, Susanne's Brother Eddie was going out with a girl in Glasgow who had a cousin coming to Australia travelling and he asked if we would consider it.

We met her in Manly and went for a bite to eat and a few drinks showing her the area, we then took her to see the apartment which she loved and said it would be great if she could stay here as it was so central and would help her find work, she had been here before with a boyfriend but they split up after three months and she went home so she had nine months left on her visa. She ended up staying the night and I dropped her off at her hostel in Sydney and would pick her up later in the day. On the way back she asked if I could stop the car and she promptly opened the door and spewed.

She became a good friend of ours and the rest of the gang at the golf club. A couple of the guys fancied her and tried to take her out, but she didn't take them up on it although she did get close to James for a while. She was invited on our weekend trips away from Sydney where we would find large houses and rent them, usually near some events that were taking place. One weekend we went to the Southern Highlands for the Bundanoon is Brigadoon event where they change the name of the train station to Brigadoon for the day and have a full Scottish Highland games programme.

Around this time I started having problems with my pissing having to get up three of four times a night going to the toilet and not being able to pass more than a dribble. I went to the doctor and was sent to see a specialist who informed me I had a growth in my prostate which luckily enough was benign but had to be operated on. I had private healthcare at this time and it all happened quickly and after the operation I was advised not to do anything for twelve weeks while my body healed. After six weeks we were painting the house with James and Claire helping and I decided I would roll the doors not thinking anything of it as I was making a healthy recovery from the operation. That night Susanne and I went for our Australian citizenship and then for a Thai meal just across the road from the flat. Next morning I got up and passed a blood clot about six inches long and one inch wide while doing the toilet and I rushed down to the doctors still in pyjamas and she told me I was very lucky and sent me for some tests. I know how lucky I was because my cousin's brother in law had the same operation and passed away with a blood clot while still in hospital. TWO LESSONS HERE: ONE IF YOU ARE HAVING PROBLEMS GET IT CHECKED AND TWO IF THEY SAY TWELVE WEEKS THEY MEAN TWELVE WEEKS.

Another trip to a house in Kiama it was decided to see how many people we could get in a shower, and it was hysterical as we were all drunk. We went to the racing at Kembla Grange on the Saturday and

I was made to spend the day doing my impersonations of Sam from the movie I am Sam and also Raymond Babbage from Rain Man and again it was a very funny day, lots of great times with Adam and Deb, James and friends that Adam and James had introduced us to Ronnie and Jenelle and Adrian and Helen.

The Hunter Valley was another stomping ground for the gang and the wineries were certainly making their money from our crowd as we went around in a minibus from winery to winery. On another occasion Susanne and I took Eddie, Angela, and Claire to the Hunter where we stayed right on the corner in amongst a lot of the wine manufacturers. We walked to the vineyards starting at the furthest away one and making our way back towards our accommodation. We got to our fifth one which was Tempus Two which was right on the opposite corner from where we were staying. It was bucketing of rain, and we decided to do a spot of lunch and a couple of bottles of wine, should have been the cue for home but no over the road to McGuigan's and more sampling, surely that is enough. In a taxi to Harrigan's pub along the road where it got messy and then back to the flats for some more, pictures will show what can be achieved in a day in the Hunter Valley.

One Easter we went to Ronnie and Jenelle's and as usual a great night was had by all, after we had been in the Spa bath for a while we all sat around the big table and for some reason known only to Adrian, he lit a napkin and ended up putting it in the citronella candle, dangerous as the house had lots of greenery around but no harm done that night. Ronnie and Jenelle went out the following Saturday shopping and when they came home their house had almost burnt to the ground due to their tumble dryer. I had given Ronnie a loan of my Guinness Book of hit music and it was one of the only things that survived although a bit damaged.

Quiet night at Ron and Jenelle's, fire table week before house fire and a previous hall party

In January 2005 I was back in the UK for meetings and Susanne and Claire headed off to Melbourne on the

Friday for the Australian Open finals and had a great weekend. They went down to support Lleyton Hewitt the Australian player and that was until they set eyes on Marat Safin and then allegiances changed and support changed to the big handsome Russian who beat Hewitt in the final.

On the 26th January 2024 Susanne and I were walking up Wellington Street in Glasgow when we bumped into Claire who we had lost touch with around ten years earlier, it was a crazy meeting in the street bearing in mind that it was Australia day and nineteen years to the day when they both went to Melbourne for the tennis. Numbers were exchanged and I am sure we won't lose contact again.

Claire did do a couple of jobs for three months at a time one of which was Taronga Zoo which she loved and had many photographs taken with the animals. She also went travelling in between and went to places we have never been like Broome in Western Australia and Ayers Rock in the middle of the country.

One day we all got dressed up and went to the races at Royal Randwick near Bondi, we were beautiful if I say so myself, Eddie and I resplendent in our Scotland Jumpers and kilts. On the way up the escalator a crowd of girls were whistling and shouting at us about our kilts, I lifted mine to reveal no underwear and they kept shouting and with the warning from Susanne ringing in my ear I turned and faced them from the top of the escalator, the police were good and just advised us not to do it again.

Susanne, Claire and I went to the Mardi gras in Sydney and it was great sight to see, people of all genders in each other's toilets and people standing around on top of roof canopies and any other viewing area they could get to. We had vodka and mixers in bottles and used these up well as the pubs were mobbed, Claire had a light lollipop which she was using as a microphone and interviewing some of the people in and around the parade, you will see this in picture format.

Tempus Two winery in the rain, Harrigans pub and Sus and Claire

Raceday, Me, Claire, Eddie, Angela, Johnny, Sus,
Mardi Vodka, Claire interview and rear view

Claire went home and sent us a toy turtle called Terry with a tartan tie which we traded for a few years with different stories about where Terry had been. One of the times we were home she brought Terry and another toy turtle telling us that Terry had married, it was a good cheap laugh that lasted a while.

Our last trip with us staying in Sydney was to Vanuatu a small island three hours from Australia and still set in its way in many areas. We had two houses near each other on the Poppy's on the Lagoon resort which was stunning, and it was Adam and Deb's second baby Max first holiday abroad, and it was a great time. We went on one of the island trips and it was into the woods where the guide told us the people had been cannibals until 1968 but still some had not taken up the law. They put me at the front of the tour and as were heading to the entertainment site a tribe jumped out of the bushes and frightened the shit out of everyone but especially me as they had grabbed me and made it clear I had the most meat. Luckily all part of the entertainment and a very enjoyable day. We used to get minibus taxis all over the island, the drivers of these vehicles had unfortunately not heard of deodorant yet and Jenelle spent every journey head hanging out of the window. There was a wedding taking place on the lagoon and it was a Scottish couple in full regalia and previously mentioned Terry the Turtle made an appearance. The boys used to sit on the veranda and put the world to rights, we called this the shit trail as it started off sensible then deteriorated. I had decided that I wasn't doing my usual mental things on the way back from holiday and arrived at the airport after only a few drinks at the resort. The flight was delayed four hours and guess what, full of the chemicals again. On the plane I had my swimming goggles on swimming up and down the plane and because of the shape your eyes go with those things on the gang were calling me Mr Nagamoto and a lot of people on the plane were in hysterical laughter, idiot again.

Smelly welcome, my cannibal tribe, Terry at the Scottish wedding and on the shit trail

The job was going well and it was decided I should move to Brisbane where the head office was and made more sense rather than commuting regularly for meetings as it is a 1 hour flight between the cities.

I was travelling up to Brisbane and staying with my cousin Sadie and her husband Gary and family and house hunting on the Saturday. One weekend Susanne came with me and we see a few we liked, one in price range was in a street called Frampton and one out of price range was in Flemington Close. As we were at Frampton the paperwork was being prepared for a sale which was a real pain as we liked it. During the week Sadie called and said that one of the houses we had seen had fallen through as buyer could not get finance, I called Susanne and told her Frampton had fallen through but it was in fact Flemington which had fallen through. A kiwi couple with four boys and twins due very soon had bought a new place and we managed to get the house for less than we would have paid for the other which was a real bargain.

The furniture left Sydney and we hired a campervan to move delicate and personal belongings, when I say hired it was a scheme where you paid very little as the company wanted the thing back where it originated from and so we paid $25 and had to put some diesel in it but hey bargain. Our plan was to take our time and spend 2 nights getting there which meant we would still have the van back on time as agreed. We booked a night in what we thought was a motel with a spa bath in Nelson Bay, on the way we went and got some wine and an Indian curry. When we got to the address it turns out it was someone's house and I told Susanne that I wasn't going in there with the curry and the red wine (remember the murder in Aberdeen). She went to the door and it turns out it was a separate part of the house with a large living area and three big bedrooms off it as well as a huge kitchen and nobody else was there, throw in the spa bath out on the balcony and here I come. In the morning the woman came into the place with freshly baked bread and sat and had a chat with us and it was excellent, all in all a fantastic experience.

Next stop Byron Bay where the exact opposite was the verdict. The place we were in was a caravan park with some static mobile homes which one of them we stayed in. It wasn't the cleanest and the spa bath was in a bit of a state. We had to go out and get something to eat and the customary wine. We passed by a guy lying on the pavement with his two mates hanging over him, it looked like he was having a fit or had taken something that had disagreed with him. We swiftly moved on and in the bus shelter was a beggar in his blanket asking us for money and we hadn't even walked that far. As we got into town we ordered pizza and I told Susanne we should get some money out of the bank for tomorrow but near the bank was a café with outdoor seating and two guys were shouting at each other and obviously stoned. I was taking the money out and Susanne was panicking and she kept grabbing my arm to get away quickly which we did, leaving the bank card in the machine. Next morning we got up and hunted all over for the card before the realisation of what had happened. I phoned my cousin who worked for the Commonwealth Bank and that was who we had used and she told me that if the card is not taken in 30 seconds it gets swallowed back in to the machine. We arrived in Brisbane with no card and only the $100 I had taken out the night before. It took a week so we had to keep borrowing from my favourite family member that I knew in Brisbane.

The house we moved into was four bedroom house with pool and cost us thirty thousand dollars less than the two bedroom apartment we left in Sydney. Cheryl and Mirren came to see us when she was six month old and obviously didn't remember it, they came back when Mirren was two and a half and she remembers bits and pieces.

Uncle Daniel and Auntie Jean had immigrated aged 71, they had been a few times and it was a big party all the time, well for Daniel anyway as Auntie Jean never touched alcohol. Daniel is my dad's brother and Sadie's father. The Duff family had a great reputation for having fun especially when they were all together at my gran's house, five boys and 4 girls all with similar sense of humour led to some great times. While I didn't get to spend much time with my dad I did get a great nearly ten years in the company of Uncle Daniel and we had so many laughs together. From Paisley just outside Glasgow he was a St Mirren supporter all his days until he got roped in to rugby league and he loved it. He was in my golf club tipping competition in Sydney and all the guys used to have a go at me saying he was imaginary and I was running the competition they thought I was at it. All the guys (all Australians) used to meet on a Friday night at the golf club and stand around at the table, it was called column eight after a newspaper sports column and they would put the world to rights. Daniel won the competition and they were all shouting fix and who is Daniel. I responded with he is a 75 year from just outside Glasgow who has only known about Rugby League for a couple of years and he has whipped every one of your arses, great work my man.

Uncle Daniels twin sister Barbara (Babs) and her daughter Carole came to stay for a few days and I took Babs for a game of golf, she had taken it up in her late sixties and was coming along but she thoroughly enjoyed it and it gave us some good quality family time together. We also had a helicopter trip booked around Sydney and that was fantastic as you will see from the photos on the next page were taken with a four megapixel Sony Cybershot through the glass floor of the helicopter. The briefing was painful as the guy told us if we landed on water we only had ten seconds to get out and that the rotor being the heaviest part of the whole thing it would flip easily, however he did say he had no intention of landing on the water. As we were getting in he leaned over and said to Susanne to hold on tight as her door latch wasn't the best, again you will see from one of the pictures she did not enjoy it one bit.

Our helicopter, me, Susanne, Auntie Babs and Carole, door doesn't close right, Harbour Bridge and Opera House from helicopter

When I had arrived in Australia on the Sunday and I had moved in to the flat I would go for a walk along Manly Beach and then in for dinner flicking through the channels and came across State of Origin which is a rugby league match between people who were born in Queensland or New South Wales, it was special because you could be playing with someone from your team in normal matches but against them in State of Origin. I watched the first of three games and was hooked, it is not so bad nowadays but used to be a brutal affair with fights all over the pitch, a great sporting event indeed. If I was working away Susanne would go around and watch it with Daniel, who loved his whisky and poor Susanne would need to join in, she would struggle to make work next morning. They play three games in the series over a six week period so it was a rough time for Susanne. He also loved when we would take him out for the Melbourne Cup, he loved his racing too and we would end up playing the poker machines in the pub or club and either taxi home or Sadie or Gary would pick us up.

I was the sixth employee of Rain Harvesting and we ended up growing to fifty four with myself looking after all the major accounts. I got on well with everyone until one night we had a company get together, I was just back from the birth of grand-daughter Mirren and told Gareth it was tough leaving her behind. He turned to a guy who had just started with us and told him that I was not the type of employee he needed and life became tough for the next six months. The guy he told left a week later.

I used to do a trip flying in to Cairns on the Sunday and working my way back down to Mackay for the Friday. Susanne would fly up on the Friday afternoon and we would spend the weekend in and around the area. One time we stayed at a place called Blacks Beach, a beautiful spot right on the water with a massive beach across the bay. On the Saturday morning we went around to the beach and took breakfast and newspapers for me to pick my horses. We sat down and started to enjoy and it was getting very warm so I went in for a dip in fact I went in a few times and then it got too warm and we went back to the apartment. In the afternoon we were going for a walk before going out when we saw the sign that says please do not swim in these waters as the water is loaded with box jellyfish which are deadly.

I went on another trip to a golf outing in Melbourne with our biggest customer Bunnings and played a round at a beautiful course called Cape Shank which was most enjoyable. Next day we were playing Moonah Links which is a brilliant links course in the Mornington Peninsula where some of the best courses in the world reside. We got off the coach and were told to go to the safety briefing, instead four of us went to the bar. We teed off and it was very windy, well what do you expect from a links course. We had taken a few beers each with us and ignored the drinks cart until we stood on the fourteenth tee and the drinks cart came around. We stopped it this time and the girl looked at my socks which were full of bindies (sticky willies in Scotland), she asked if we had went to the briefing and asked if we had been in the long grass, I told her I had been nowhere else but the long grass. She pulled out two clipboards, one with a picture of tiger snakes and one of black snakes with the instruction do not go in the long grass as the course is loaded with deadly snakes. I know how to live dangerous but played the rest of the course with my putter.

My leaving Rain Harvesting was made easier due to a catastrophic event that happened in January 2011. The rains came and in a big way culminating in 75% of the state of Queensland flooded. Thirty three people lost their lives and three remained unaccounted for presumed dead. The floods were bad enough but the local Dam overflowed as well causing huge swelling in the Brisbane River. Cheryl and baby Mirren were with us at the time and all we could do was sit and watch on TV as the situation unfolded. One incident saw a huge walkway breakaway and heading for a collision with the Gateway bridge which is the main arterial road to and from the airport but the genius of a tug boat operator turned it and guided it through the pillars and out to sea. As we sat watching TV a structure went by on the river and I turned to Susanne and the kids and told them that what was on the screen was where I had booked for next Sunday lunch, the Drift restaurant was very well named as it drifted down the Brisbane River. It was a horrible event but one which led to me being made redundant as it is pretty difficult to sell rainwater products in floods and the drought was broken in a big way all throughout Australia.

We took a holiday back to Scotland before I went to look for another job and while home we went out with wee Bobby, he was a friend and ex colleague of Susanne's who had fallen on a bit of hard times although he stayed in a homeless unit he was always immaculately dressed. We used to meet him and take him for a few beers and drop him a few quid. We met him and we went to the Heilin Jessie pub near the Glasgow Barra's markets. We told him we had moved to Queensland and he asked where as he had family there, we told him Capalaba and he says that is where my sister lives and he got out his little book and said he was wrong it was Alexandra Hills, our house was the boundary between the two suburbs and we found out who his sister was. When we went home we had lunch at Sadie's and gave her the names Cecilia and John and she had known them for thirty years and that they were all members of the Capalaba Soccer Club where her son Barry had played. She said if we wanted to introduce ourselves the father (Papa) and mother (Annie) of the family go to the Capalaba Tavern on a Saturday to watch the racing and have a bet, she told me we would recognise them with the accent and also that Papa had early onset of Parkinson's disease. We went on the Saturday and there was a woman sitting at one of the tables and then Papa walked around the bar towards her. I was standing next to Susanne but shouting at here to ask what she wanted to drink hoping the accent might be recognised and communications begin, but nope. After a short while we walked over and asked if they were John and Anna and in her best Glasgow accent Anna said "who the fuck is asking", welcome to the Quinn family. When we told her I was Sadie from the banks cousin things mellowed a bit and we were invited to the club on the Sunday.

The club opened around 2pm on the Sunday and closed around 8.00pm and it was pool competition day, I took part and won which didn't go down great as the family were staunch Catholics and were beaten by the wee protestant guy, but it soon became clear we would all be friends.

There were four brothers in Australia, John, Willie Paul and Tony and one sister still in Scotland Rosemary. When we were home one time Henry told us he was seeing a girl from Maryhill and it turns out it was Rosemary, they didn't go out for long, not sure what happened there. The boys had all played for the Capalaba team over the years and John I believe was by far the best and he was still playing a bit into his fifties.

The club became a regular haunt for us on the Sunday and I transformed the pool tournament by simply taking over the running of it, if there were twelve players they would get down to six and then three with someone getting a bye into the final. Simple solution play four games with four byes and then down to eight, four and then two.

Back to the music, Susanne and I had booked to go and see Maroon 5 in Brisbane and we booked into a plush hotel and early evening we had a Japanese banquet, we then left to go to the Convention Centre just across the bridge, when we got there it was very quiet and we walked all around the building before checking the tickets and the concert was in the Entertainment Centre thirty minutes away. As we were walking back across I got a phone call from Cheryl from the back of an Ambulance with her appendix burst, turns out she was fine but no way that we were going to any concert. We still have the tickets and tell people we have them and ask if they would like to go and see them but think the 2007 date on the tickets might put them off! We also went to see Pink and that again was a great concert, she is some performer and singer.

I had joined Redland Bay Golf Club a very picturesque club and played alongside Greg (Australian) Gary (Australian) and Dave (English). We played normally early Saturday mornings to avoid the heat and every week at the 16th tee I would give them their Scottish fact for the week, it would be along the lines of "that tarmac you are walking on, Scottish, "the tyres on your buggy, Scottish" "Waltzing Matilda, Scotsman" but best one ever was "Speedo's swimwear, Scotsman". After the round we would have a couple of light beers then home. I would go for a shower and then a nap and Susanne and I would go out for the day to various places around the area including the beautiful Raby Bay area which had a few bars and plenty restaurants. We ended up moving to Cleveland and we were 100m walk to this area which was amazing. One of the guys in the club Joe used to live in Hobart and tells the story when the large American aircraft carrier USS Ulysses came to the area, Joe had a boat and a friend asked if he could bring some people on to the boat and he agreed. The guy turns up with a load of scantily clad girls with signs and when all the sailors were around the rails on the ship the girls stripped and held up signs for a strip club in Hobart, Joe was mortified but worse was to follow as the six o'clock news came on and Joe's daughter a news reporter was telling the whole of Australia about the Americans visitors when Joe's boat comes in to view with certain parts of ladies anatomy blacked out.

It was around this time I was nearing my 50th birthday and was sure the family would be planning something special around the day. About four weeks before my boss Murray asked if I could go and look at a resort on the Gold Coast and also a Golf Club down there where we were going to entertain customers, I am the man for the job, he told me I could take Susanne too and they were arranging for me to golf with the professional and I had to wear all my Rain Harvesting work clothes for photographs and other promotional purposes.

On the Wednesday before we are due to go down Susanne says that she and Sadie are going to the Karaoke at the Alexandra Hills Hotel and Gary will come around and play a few games of pool, table in the garage. After a few hours Susanne comes in and says right Gary Sadie is waiting outside in the car, he ups and goes, I tell Susanne that they are both ignorant buggers the way they left, no more thought of it.

On the Friday I am driving down the coast when Murray phoned going over all that was happening, got it boss. When we arrived Susanne says she will collect the keys while I park the car and we go to the apartment 1 floor up overlooking the pool, good start. I pour the drinks and put on some music which Susanne turns up loud, I tell her there are other people in the complex and we do not want any complaints especially with it being a works thing. Ten minutes later and the door chaps, see I told you, open the door and there is Adam and Deb, Ronnie and Jenelle and James and Marnie up from Sydney, Adrian and Helen and Johnny arrive later. I am now starting to get the picture.

Saturday morning we go to play golf at Robina Woods and come back in the afternoon where a barbecue is set up by the pool, now we have Sadie and Gary and Susanne's boss Bo, Shaz and Alyssa also up from Sydney. Well at least she managed to get my new golf bag as the big box in the corner has my name on it. I was asked to open the presents first and just as I get to the box up jumps Cheryl, she was the reason for the secrecy on the Wednesday as she had arrived from

Scotland then. Apologies to my cousin and her husband and it turns out this was all part of operation Murray devised by Susanne. I swore for years that no one would ever catch me out but here I was stitched up like a kipper but what a great weekend.

50th Mission accomplished, my caricature, Ron, Jennelle, Sadie, Gary and Cheryl out of the box

Helen, Adrian and Johnny, James, Marnie and
baby Emily, Deb and Adam and Max and Deb

I got another job with a company called Infastech who specialised in Industrial fasteners for various industries but biggest was Rail which they used heavy duty two piece fasteners for sleepers on the Rail lines, these were called Huck Bolts and needed special tooling to put the fastener and the collar together. I was called to a job in the middle of nowhere and got there early and was walking around and went under a bridge and right up above me was metal plates with the name Motherwell Bridge on them felt proud that product manufactured in Scotland was here.

I went with a colleague called Peter to the mining show in Mackay in mid north Queensland in which we were displaying our products. We were due to stay in a cabin outside Mackay but in the weeks before it had rained heavily and the cabin ended up being isolated and we tried for a Motel but to no avail as the place was packed for the show. We ended up in a tented village near the show but more importantly right next to Mackay Airport where they started the engines at 4.00am and started flying around 5.00am and no matter how much we had to drink we were wakened from that time in the morning.

While working for this company I started talking to a company called Crimsafe who made safety screens for doors and windows to a very high standard. In Australia people leave their doors open to let in air and let heat out and these screens allowed that to happen whilst providing high levels of security. They had a security screw made for them and supplied by a small company on the Gold Coast where they were based. I introduced them to rivet systems which could seriously speed up production and still providing the security, we started testing and the first couple of goes were not great however we kept trying and eventually we provided what seemed a better solution. At this time we were bought over by the Stanley Engineered Fastening Group and told that everything would be the same. The test that they done in-house was to hit the screen with a large piece of four by two timber with a guy at each side slamming it into the screen, best attempt was twenty two hits before the mesh started to come away from the screen. Next was the big test, they were trying to repel a force of 700 joules and we went to the Australian National University in Canberra where they set up the screen and fired a cannonball at it, very impressive very noisy even with ear muffs on but the screen remained intact. Next they wanted to try twelve hundred joules, ear muffs back on and bang, the cannonball went straight through, still the seven hundred was where they had their specification and we were now starting to talk Commercials.

We were in the early quoting stages and they had suggested that they would probably like to look at Dewalt screwdrivers and tooling for all their subcontractors throughout Australia and possibly North America as well as they were spreading their wings. The Managing Director of Stanley Engineered Fastening came up from Melbourne and I done a presentation backed up by him about the support we could offer around all the states of Australia and we were a global company and that would work well.

In early January I was on my way to meet with them to discuss the quote when I stopped at the petrol station off the highway, I got petrol and decided to have a sausage roll for lunch as I was nice and early. I got the sausage roll and tomato sauce and just in time remembered my breakfast experience on the plane with yoghurt all over me, took the sauce held it away, pressed the two ends and it squirted all over the place, not over me but an elderly woman sitting behind me with a white top on. A couple of people seen this and were laughing but I had to go up and confess which I did, they were on a bus tour and she took it well and I decided to go an buy them a load of chocolate and when I got back they were all gone, so I was lumbered with a load of chocolate on a stinking hot Queensland day, I gave it all away to a group of school kids but I think they were already melting, the chocolates not the kids.

The meeting went very well and I came out with a verbal agreement to supply all the fasteners and order would be for over $900,000 which came through a couple of days later, this was without the tooling that we were looking at for them. Early February I was trying to fix a rivet tool that wasn't my job but I had been given all the gear to do it from my predecessor and a manual of how to do it by head office, however in doing this work I dislocated my shoulder. I was going to be off for a while and come March they made me redundant and excuse was that the Tooling specialist in the area would look after the account and he was based in Sydney. I spoke with Ramesh from Crimsafe who I was dealing with a bit later and he told me they had pulled the plug on the deal as the MD had promised local coverage and national coverage and had taken me out of the equation. They never bought the fasteners and decided to go with another tooling supplier too, good on them.

We had a trip home booked and I was travelling with my arm in a sling and as you can guess it wasn't a very pleasant flight as I could not get comfortable at all for the full duration of the flight. When back at Susanne's mums she had a big chair with wide arms and I spent a few nights sleeping as best as I could sitting up. After a few days I noticed that my ankles and legs had blown up a lot more than normal from travelling and I had to go to the doctors and explain how I had been living. He gave me a prescription for tablets and told me I had to lie down and make sure my ankles and bottom of my legs were above my heart, well took tablet and lay down as suggested and ten minutes later came the first of a thousand pee's over the next couple of days, legs were fine after that but I was knackered because every time I was going to sleep I had to get up to go the toilet, nightmare trip all in all.

I put a claim in against the company and they made me a rubbish offer, I had presented to the lawyer pictures of the tooling in my garage and the manual and she pushed them and I end up getting a better deal and my shoulder healed up after a long time in physiotherapy and cortisone injections.

I had a couple of jobs that were very short term, both around six months. I joined Specifix Fasteners which was a division of Ajax Fasteners based in Melbourne and I was reporting to Julie who could put Scottish people to shame with her swearing indeed she was a master of the c... word which is generally never used by women. I then joined a company called Nordale which specialised in adhesives and EVA used for Ugg boot manufacturing which was big on the Gold Coast. We also supplied a Yacht manufacturer on the Gold Coast with 20L drums of glue and we were constantly on stop credit with suppliers. We nearly stopped production a few times and one of them I came into branch to see Russell (38 years' service) loading his car with 20 drums of the glue. I told him to empty his car and he told me he done this a lot and I went nuts, the glue was highly flammable and could explode at any time in high heat or if someone crashed in to him. He fell out with me and left a few months in to my tenure. The stop credit was driving me crazy as it was constant and the guy who owned it did not appreciate the issues and eventually I had a major row with him when he was next in Queensland and I resigned, He had to do me a leaving form and put reason for leaving as dereliction of duties.

I got a call from Sean who I worked with at Infastech and he had joined a company called Festo who were German manufacturers of Pneumatic equipment based in Brisbane. I went for the interview and got on well with Kevin who was the boss for Queensland. I was called back for a second interview with Kevin and Sean and was offered the role of account manager.

I had never had any dealings with Pneumatics before and I really struggled with the concepts, Kevin I am sure was regretting ever having crossed me but I persevered because Sean had given me the opportunity and I didn't want to let him down. Every night I went home Susanne told me to leave but I was determined and spent a lot of time with Kevin training. While I was not a Pneumatics expert I was a salesman and started to bring in new business then one day it clicked, it was a eureka moment and from then on I got it. I then went on to enjoy my time at Festo and worked with a great group of people and it was easily my second best job behind Kleeno the clown.

Cheryl and Mirren came again and we celebrated Mirren's 5th birthday in Cleveland, she remembers some of this trip and especially about the warhead sweets she used to trick us with. These were mental and burned your mouth when taken, good laughs for her but dangerous for everyone else. It was during this trip that we had decided we should go back home to Scotland to be nearer family, a big decision but one we had spoken about but had never put a date on it.

We had bought a flat in Cleveland and sold the house with pool early September. The flat was being rented out as a holiday accommodation mainly for people visiting their families from the UK and it worked out a lot cheaper than hotels or motels. When we bought it was renting for nine hundred dollars a week but it was only rented for one week September, 1 week October, 1 week November and three weeks in December to a family who came every year to see their family. The people who were buying our house were not in any hurry to move in so we decided we would move January. We decided that it would be best if we moved in to Cleveland to save extra costs and contacted the Estate Agent, she said she would notify the people concerned and she was very sad that the family who came every year would miss out, this was on the Friday and on the Monday the agent called to confirm she had cancelled however she told us that they had two enquiries one for three weeks October and three weeks November, too good to miss out on that, so told her to tell the people the crazy Scotsman had made a mistake and all of sudden we were nearly fully booked so we decided to book a holiday back to Scotland from 28th December. We had a cage downstairs in the garage area where we kept things and one day I needed access but the key to the padlock was on the bunch of keys. I chapped the door and a guy opened it and asked how you doing Terry and I said fine Michael, turns out it was my accountant who had rented out his large property while he went back to England to spend time with his sick father and the flat was a perfect interim solution for him.

A year later we went back to Scotland for Xmas and New Year and partied the whole time, we were returning on the tenth January early morning and next afternoon going on a cruise around the Barrier Reef with the Quinn's. We got on the boat and were all told about the safety briefing which was held on the side of the boat. John and Cecilia had told Papa and Anna to stay indoors as they were not the most mobile by this time, however one of the stewards opened the door and was trying to chase them out, nobody knew what had happened until Cecilia's friend who was waving us off sent her a message to say Anna was out on the walkway, no way says Cecilia but when Agnes sent a picture we knew it was true. After the briefing we spent the first hour of the cruise wandering around looking for Anna, eventually finding her. There was a good crowd of us and all had the big drinks package so we did go for it, on the first day we were sitting and Robert looked up and saw his brother Malcolm standing there, none of them knew the other was on the same cruise. One afternoon early on we were having a laugh and I saw a couple sitting behind us laughing away hysterically with us, I went over and started talking to them and turns out they were Scottish and I invited Andy and Marie to join us. We all got on great and we decided the big party would be on the Friday and not Saturday as we had to disembark early on Sunday. We had a great night and all headed to bed at roughly the same time, think it was around 3.00am. Next day we were in a bar when Andy and Marie came in and Andy told us that he had a bit of a mishap during the night, most people on cruises or hotels leave the toilet light on so that you know where you are, however Marie had turned it out and Andy got up for the toilet and went following the light, next thing he is out on the corridor with the door locked behind him bollock naked. He tried to waken Marie but with no luck, not to worry the female security guard who turned up could help but she didn't have the master key, not to worry the other female security guard could help and she let him in. Andy trusted in us and told us not to tell the others which we told him we wouldn't, this deserves a smile at this time. We went in to the main hall to watch the cabaret when the gentlemen hosting mentioned he had a special mention for Andy and everyone in the place already knew, he didn't even need to tell the story. A few weeks later when I was in at my customer Honeywell I bumped in to Andy, didn't know he worked there but was still smiling. We did go out with them a couple of times back in Glasgow and still keep in touch.

We had quite a few visitors over our time in Australia and Bud, Margaret, Wee Bud and Martin came to Brisbane as well as Sydney and had a great time, they done all the tourist stuff and spent lots of time in the pool, Wee Bud also showed me how to open my garage door from the inside which I couldn't do before. Billy and Rita came for their 25th Wedding anniversary and my Australian family made a big fuss over them which was great. We went down to Sydney, they stayed fifty five floors up near Darling Harbour and we went to see their room, as mentioned before I am not the best with heights and made the stupid mistake of saying this to Billy and the big shit jumped up and down in the lift for all fifty five floors. We went to Royal Randwick races and Billy picked the first winner called our Joan of Arc which was the school that their daughter Jacqueline had attended. I didn't get a chance to explain how the betting worked in Australia before he put the bet on, but who cares when you pick a 50/1 winner. He picked the next three winners and was slagging me rotten but revenge was to come in the form of the sixth race of the day, I had been going on about the Snowden trained horse all day. Race due off bet on and confidence high, strike the front run away with it yes you beauty, go to window to collect and had put the wrong number down, another DOH! We left on the Sunday and they went to Manly and had a great time in the Steyne pub as Manly won the rugby League Grand Final forty nil.

Susanne's friend from her work at Fyfe and McGrouther, Margaret and her husband Dennis came over also, the pair had met in Blackpool both there on long weekends with respective friends and got married a short time later. She is from Glasgow, he is from Leeds and they done the sensible thing and settled in Wales.

One time Eddie came on his own and we took him to the Rugby League match between Brisbane Broncos and the Queensland Cowboys at Suncorp Stadium, he was amazed that you could sit and drink during the game, by this time I was becoming an expert on the game or so I told Eddie. It was the first game of the season and it finished 40-40 and on leaving I told him that none of those two would be anywhere near the grand final. 2015 grand final Broncos 16 v Cowboys 17 the game was won by a golden point in overtime scored by Jonathan Thurston who I deem to be the best player I had seen but there were a few really good competitors for that mantle. I was at a function when another great Wally Lewis was the guest speaker, he moved to England and was the highest paid player in the league, and he told how during play even his own team mates would swing away at him when they were scrapping for possession. Another time Eddie and mum came and they went with Susanne to a Celtic convention night in Brisbane where they met the famous Willie Wallace who was one of the players to be the first British team to win the European Cup in 1967.

On the 1st of February 2016 Susanne got a call to say that mum was unwell and was needing looked after, both the boys were working and it was getting tough, mum was 80 at the time and her little body was not supporting her mental strength. Susanne flew out that night and that was our last night staying together in our flat. I arranged to rent out the flat and not knowing if we would be back or not. I had a lovely evening with the family on the Thursday and after my farewell party at Festo which were both very tearful, I left Australia on 22nd July 2016.

Susanne stayed with mum and I moved back in to the old house in Moodiesburn which Eddie still owned and he moved in with his bride to be Heather. It was good being back in the old house but it was a long way from all my friends in Yoker. I used to get an all-day bus ticket and go there at weekends, it would be a bus to Glasgow City Centre a walk through the town and then another bus to meet the boys. My journey back was slightly different as I would get a bus to bottom end of town, have something from the chippy then bus to top end of town and then another bus back to Moodiesburn a bit of a trek but enjoyable and dangerous being in town alone with a drink in me.

The boys would take turns looking after mum and we managed to get some long weekends and a week away at a time. One trip we went to beautiful apartments overlooking Albufeira beach in Portugal, the complex was run by a German woman and the reception was only opened until 6.00pm, she lived off site about an hour away. We had a great break with some good food and drinks for the week. We were due to get picked up from the apartments at 6.30am and we decided last day would be down in the old town square where we had a nice dinner and started making our way back to the apartment. On our way back we decided to stop at a bar three quarters of the way up the hill called Eddie's run by a 62 year old Portugese man and his 25 year old German girlfriend. We had stopped a few times here and they introduced us to white sangria. It was decided on the way there we would have one white and one red jug of sangria, well we had two white then two red then the couple got us on to shots and then we had Drambuie as night caps and by now it is well after twelve and we still had a bottle of wine in the room. We got to the outside door and I opened with the card, we then went to the lift and stepped in and turned around to talk to each other but bumped and the card went flying in the air and straight down the gap between the lift and the landing!!!! We had been model guests all week but now we had to phone the German woman and get her out of her bed and as you can guess she was not pleased when she got to us around one thirty am, oh well these things happen don't they.

You've read about the 40th and the 50th birthdays well here comes the 60th, Susanne had asked me what I wanted to do for this and I politely suggested a trip to the Melbourne Cup would be sufficient, what we stayed there all that time and you never wanted to go there, well it was time now. So we spoke with friends in Sydney and they agreed a great idea and we would all meet in Melbourne. We got a great deal for flights which included Glasgow to Melbourne then Sydney then Brisbane and back to Glasgow for £866 each which when looking at these now are three and near four times this price. Helen our friend from Sydney had suggested she might like to go but it was all organised by the Sydney crew and it was decided it would not be a good idea but we would go and stay with her when we got to Sydney.

This trip included a trip to one of the most famous horse races in the world and also would be known as the bad feet break. We checked into the hotel which was a real nice place on the Saturday morning and went for a walk around Melbourne which was nice but I had new shoes on and when walking up the stairs Susanne noticed that my heels were covered in blood and I had removed several layers of skin, ouch. I managed to get a pair of sandals on after that but they then cut my toes and my feet were in a state. The troops from Sydney arrived on the Sunday and we had a lovely meal and great laughs with all the gang back together. I happened to mention to James and Adam that the hotel was lovely and both together in their best Australian accents said what a tit I was as this was the same one we had stayed in for the golf trip we had.

On the Tuesday morning of the cup Adam and I went for a beer at seven thirty am at a little place around the corner from the hotel and we then left around nine am for Flemington via a large limousine which took us straight in to the course. I was dressed in my full MacDuff tartan suit and Susanne looked resplendent in a beautiful dress and pacifier, she looked that well that she had her photo taken at the winning line, wait a minute it was my birthday treat, something wrong there. We were in a large hospitality tent at the back of the course and a short walk to see the races, it was torrential rain early in the morning but come the race it was as bright as anything as if God had changed the weather for the big race. The race was won by Cross Country trained by English Trainer Charlie Appleby and ridden by Australian jockey Kerrin McEvoy and all the Australians had bet it but Susanne and I didn't. Again we had some lovely food and plenty of chemical products and a bit of dancing afterwards as well before heading back to the limousine for the trip back to the hotel.

We all left on the Wednesday heading back to Sydney on various flights but when we were in the airport, Susanne dropped the bombshell that Helen did not want us to stay with her as she thought we were using her because she never got an invite to Melbourne. We slithered what response we should give her and debated screaming and bawling, saying sorry and explaining it was not us who organised the event and then I came up with the genius "OK" and that was the last we heard from her. We then booked into a hotel in Manly and enjoyed our few days there catching up with friends from work and Balgowlah Golf Club. We also had a great night with Susanne's old boss Bo and his wife Shaz, the crazy Croat and the mental Irish woman, a beautiful couple with wonderful kids.

We then headed up to Brisbane to stay with Sadie and Gary at their wonderful waterfront property in Cleveland. They had booked us a couple of days away on Stradbroke Island which is a 30 minute ferry ride from Cleveland and it is a glorious place with wonderful sights and beautiful beaches. Second day we were out exploring most of the day and had decided we would go to the bowling club for dinner and so we made our way there at approximately eight pm only to find they finished serving at the same time, we had a few drinks and went home for cereal and crisps for dinner. It was a good break and we caught up again with ex workmates and the boys from Redland Bay Golf Club.

They had also organised a day out on a boat to a beautiful spot called Peel Island where they filmed a fair bit for the Pirates of the Caribbean. The boat parked up and we had a swim and a nice lunch and then sat around having drinks, the sun was beating down and we were all coating ourselves in sunscreen, well I did but did not for my feet and after a few hours these started swelling, another foot issue on this holiday. We left a couple of days later and I travelled from Cleveland to Glasgow without any shoes on.

Gang at the races, morning of the cup, finishing line pic whose birthday is it, afternoon at the cup

MEET YRRET FFUD

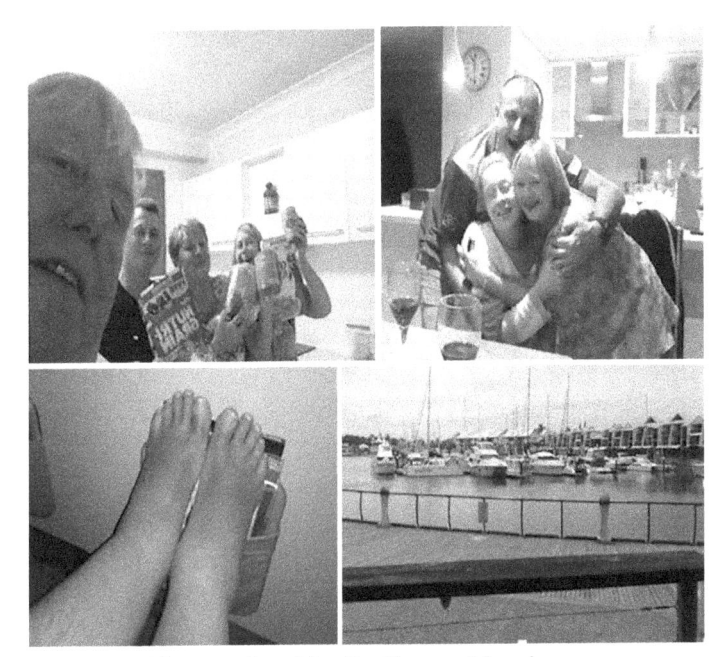

Dinner at Straddie, Bo, Shaz and Sus, home
without shoes, view from my old local

I went with the Yoker lads for a long weekend in
Benidorm, they went every year and stayed at the Perla
Hotel central to the town activities. The time I went
a few of the guys were in the Perla but the rest of us
were miles away and the Friday night was a nightmare
with us all going back separate via taxi's and so
Saturday afternoon I said I would check to see if we
could get something nearer. I typed in Perla just in

165

case it had changed overnight and lo and behold there were plenty available, how many will I get, five get five okay booked. We were in a pub right beside the Perla so we decided to give it time for the confirmation to come through and the praise to be given to hero Terry. Confirmation through and we had the rooms booked at the Perla in Rome, DOH! I got on it pretty quick and did get full refund and we managed to find some rooms around about and a two apartment for Tony and me. This was a complete booze fest and recently has died away as I think a lot of the guys cannot handle it anymore.

When I returned in 2016 I had brought Uncle Daniels bowls with me and I joined the Yoker Bowling Club and started to try and play, he was a big tall man and his bowls were size six and kept falling out of my hands so I bought some size fours which suited better. I had an operation on my left hand for a thing called Dupytrans contractions where the tendons thicken on the palm and pull the fingers down. Now the right hand both the pinkie and finger next to it had started to do the same, I then went down to a borrowed size two bowl and that worked ok and would do until I had my second operation which I had in 2022. In February 2019 Susanne and I went to Las Vegas with Billy, Rita and Jacqueline, before I left I was asked if I would help out with the board of directors and I said okay. The Annual General Meeting took place in

February when we were away and when I came back I was Vice President how the hell did that happen. Next February I was President and had to see the club through the Co-vid pandemic which was tough but with the support of the other guys especially Gary Earl who applied for every grant that was available we done it. Last thing I had done was a clear out of the locker room which was in a bit of a mess and there were many sets of bowls from members who had been dead for many years. In doing this I came across a bag which I recognised which was a Bunnings Australia tool bag and it had a set of size two bowls in it, I asked around and not one person knew where they had come from or who they belonged too so I am now the proud owner of a set of bowls that had been to Australia for some sort of holiday. During this clean-up we came across bowls trophies dating back to the 1890's, these were old wooden bowls with plaques on them identifying the winner and the year. The club was founded in 1850 and went through the Second World War being damaged by German bombers during the Clydebank Blitz and then a fire destroyed all the old records that were kept. We do believe that the inventor of the television John Logie Baird was a member, I had a meeting with a family whose grandfather was club champion in the 1920's and 30's and they told us that one of his best friends was the said inventor who we know lived in the street next to the club. The club is now down to 40 odd members and celebrates 175 years in 2025 and planning some special events throughout the year. In 2018 Jim came across from Canada and we had a good night together and got the same photograph taken that we had done forty years before.

In September of 2018 Cheryl gave birth to her son Mason for the wee perfect family along with Mirren who is really into her dancing and doing well at school. Mason will play for Rangers, all he talks about and plays is football, when he was four he was rhyming off all the famous players like Ronaldo, Messi, Lewandowski and I remind him when I was four I could hardly talk. Great kids and watching them grow is amazing.

I am still working at age sixty five and due to retire in December 2024 but not sure about that as I enjoy being a Key Account Manager for Aerospace customers in Scotland but will see how my health holds up, my hands have healed and I am still bowling although considering going back to golf. When I joined Cromwell I was in a branch training and met Alistair McKay who was internal sales, I told him we had bought a house from someone called McKay and he asked if it was in Dykebar Avenue and I said yes, it was his auntie's old house, just another coincidence. Susanne's mum is still with us at this time and we are still managing to get the odd break away with the boys looking after mum. Eddie and Heather eventually got married after the wedding being postponed twice during Co-vid and it was a great day in a sensational chapel St Mary's in Carlton and a great reception in the Glasgow Central Hotel. The family surprised the happy couple with a visit from the singing waiters, this is a company who send in people dressed as waiters and one drops cutlery and next minute they all pull out microphones and burst into song, great entertainment.

Back to the music this time in and around Glasgow, I saw people like Sparks doing promotional tours, they would play a few songs and then answer some questions from the crowd. On the day I saw them they were throwing albums into the crowd and I managed to get my hands on a bit of it and another guy had a bit but loads of people trying to get it, it seemed me and one other guy were in the lead and I swung and stuck one on his chin and he staggered back and I won. James Haffie I apologise for the punch but I wanted the album, James stayed just around the corner from me. Suzi Quatro, the Arrows and Smokie were all on RAK records and done a co tour. Status Quo numerous times but one of the best was the Sensational Alex Harvey Band at the Apollo in Glasgow and it was his last in his home city, he had a character called Vambo and he used to start the gig by coming through a brick wall with Vambo spray painted on it. He crashed through the wall and I think they had used better concrete as he seemed to hurt himself and said he wasn't going to crash through walls no more, he retired and died not long after. The latest we saw in Glasgow were Simply Red and Jeff Lynne's ELO and all were excellent.

Well we are almost up to date but just one more story to relay and it is not about me but my hero Alexander Stuart Duff.

Alexander Duff, the man who brought to life the "wen we wur wee" series of short stories about his memories of growing up in Whiteinch. Alexander was born in Alexandria Dunbartonshire on the 9th January 1951 the third of six boys. He was born with the debilitating illness Muscular Dystrophy (An inherited disorder characterised by progressive muscular weakness).The family moved to Whiteinch when Alexander was young however most of his early life was spent in Mearnskirk hospital where he was under constant testing of new potential cures for the disease.

Alexander's muscles were not so strong in his legs so the times he was home he was fitted with callipers to try and support his walking. He destroyed many of these callipers playing around the close, the bins, the dunny and the gangway. All the parents and families in the area loved him, young and old kids admired him because he had a go at everything everyone else was doing. Climbing and sliding off the dykes that housed the rubbish bins, Cowboys and Indians and many more. He claimed to be the area's best faller because he did it that much. Hide and seek was a big favourite, if he fell going to hide he would crawl into the bins or round the back of them, he was good at that game... He was actually the dirtiest wean out of them aw ma maw would say. He wasn't seen as disabled but more as a cheery wee soul giving everything he could.

Alexander would disappear for hours on end to Victoria Park where many adventures from his stories were played out with his mates, you know them, Stinky, Spoon and McCluskey were the main ones, and they would take him there in their bogey and play for hours and hours even in the dark.

Alexander was nine and still in and out of hospital when we moved to Knightswood, the Clyde Tunnel project was well underway that was why we had to move. Life was exciting here too as we had a large area behind the house to play and also the Garscadden burn ran through it, while all the other kids would jump the burn Alexander would just walk through it. He took part in all the games, football which he was good at and had excellent close control, cricket, and rugby and still played cowboys and Indian's.

He went to Rottenrow School in Townhead and the bus would pick him up and drop him off. He liked school a lot and would talk loads and loads about it when he got home at 4.00pm. An hour later and the nurse would show up to give him his daily injection.

When he left school he got a job in Singers sewing machine factory in Clydebank where he was for a few years working as a needle engineer, his job was to straighten the needles and it was piece work so the more you done over a certain number the more you got paid. He had himself a little blue disabled car which was a three wheeler which you weren't supposed to take passengers in. He used to get one of the guys to load it up with boxes of needles which he would bring home and his three younger brothers also became needle engineers but somehow never saw much of the bonus.

When he was twenty he went with my dad to the pub and saw a guy win a bottle of whisky in a darts competition, my dad said he wished he had won it as he liked whisky, which triggered the efforts of the next eight years.

The dartboard was bought probably using our needle engineering bonus, it was hung up in the living room cupboard and at 6.00am every weekday morning it was thud, thud, thud, and walk to the board thud, thud, and thud until 7.30am when he went to work. When he came home at 4.30pm it was straight on the board and yes you guessed it thud, thud, thud. He was dedicated and desperate to win my dad a bottle of whisky and after a few months he went to the pub and took part in his first competition, it took a wee while before he won but dad was over the moon and this gave Alexander a non-drinker by the way the confidence to go into more competitions.

He started playing team darts locally in the Clydebank and District League playing for the Burgh bar and playing in competitions throughout the area. He went to play in an open competition in a very famous darts pub on the South side of Glasgow which he won and he was invited to join the team of the Sou Wester bar who had International players in their team including one of the most famous called Harry Heenan. He played for the team and was selected for the Glasgow team and then the Scotland team where he played his first international against England and Eric Bristow's dad George. He also played for a Great Britain team who played the rest of Europe which included a very good Swedish player called Stefan Lord who Alexander remained friends with throughout the years. He was also good friends with Welsh hero's Leighton Rees and Alan Evans who were visitors to our house when they were playing in Scotland. Alexander became Scotland's first professional darts player ahead of the famous Jocky Wilson. He also used to play charity matches to highlight awareness and raise funds for Muscular Dystrophy and was invited to Jerry Lewis telethon in the US, Jerry was the world's biggest fundraiser in the world for the disease.

He went to the US with his good friend John Preston and they toured all around the country with Alexander lined up to take on the best players each State had to offer and won a lot more than he lost. The nights playing darts were shown on the Jerry Lewis show one a week for the duration of his stay and he would often talk to Jerry on the show. He was made an honorary citizen of Baltimore during the trip and the US loved him.

Alexander's muscle problems meant he was starting to get weaker and by the time he was twenty eight he had to give up the darts after three Scotland caps and numerous trophies won.

He moved in to buying and selling and opened a stall up in the famous Glasgow Barra's markets selling darts, flights and stems which was very successful, I also used to go around the pubs on a Monday night selling them too. He then moved in to buying and selling gold when the darts scene started to deteriorate and was pretty good at that too. He would also go around the pubs and clubs at night time and play guitar and sing and I would be his roadie carrying the amp and guitar in his little blue bubble car, it was pretty crowded in there I can tell you.

His condition was worsening and eventually he would end up wheelchair bound but that didn't stop him, he would go around to the community centre in the street I was born in and teach people the guitar and tell them little stories about his childhood and again he was loved by all.

He loved his racing and would really look forward to the big festivals watching them with our brother John,

Cheltenham was his favourite and they used to treat themselves to steaks when it was on. After John passed I tried to get down a few times but couldn't as often because of work commitments.

His childhood stories turned to print on Facebook and he had over 2,000 followers from all around the world, he would write them as if he was writing them with no capitals or punctuation marks and later he would get these little stories under the title "wen we wur wee" bastard beat me to writing a book, something we had both spoken about for years. When he took unwell over 3,500 people enquired after him on his Facebook page, people who thought they knew him through his little short stories. I was with Alexander on the Tuesday of Cheltenham 2022 and he didn't seem right, we was very distant and repeating himself, he had nurses coming in a few times per day looking after him. Cheltenham finished on the Friday and I was driving on the Saturday when his son called and told me he had passed away suddenly but peacefully. When he passed in 2022 there were over 5,000 messages expressing sadness and a good few hundred asking where they could get his book? He had 300 printed and I got the first one signed by him but when I contacted the printer they could not trace it.

In 2008 Alexander was inducted into the US darts Hall of Fame, all the more amazing considering he had such a short career.

Bubble car, handsome guy, that first bottle
for my dad, another trophy

MEET YRRET FFUD

Some trophies, John, Alex and I,
Alex's book wen we wur wee, Wullie, Alex and Robie

I recently met a supplier in a coffee shop in the Polmadie area of Glasgow who had met the great comedy legend Billy Connolly in New York. Mark asked Billy if he would keep sending him and his family the Christmas cards and Billy didn't know what he was talking about, turns out Mark stayed in a house in East Kilbride that Billy's mate used to stay in and he said he would keep them coming. Whilst having a coffee and a chat in walked Craig Moore ex Rangers, John Hartson ex Celtic and another gentleman I didn't recognise. I went over to them and spoke directly to Craig saying how much I loved seeing Buffering running, he was gobsmacked as he is a part owner of the horse which raced in Australia. We went through a few races from start to finish and I think I made his day.

Susanne turned 60 during covid and decided she wanted to go on holiday to celebrate in 2024. I said no problem but when she told me where she wanted to go things were a bit strained. Turkey is a country I have never wanted to go to after the two Leeds fans were killed on a European night when they played Galatasaray and also when I watched the game the evil on the fans faces made my decision. So Turkey it was and the resort we stayed in was called Titanic, what chance did I stand, turns out it was a very nice holiday, Eddie and Heather had stayed here the previous year and recommended it. First night Susanne sees a woman sitting on her own, think her husband was at the bar or toilet, she came over and sat beside Susanne opposite me and says I know you to me. Renee stayed two doors away from Bud in Yoker and used to run around with lots of people we knew, her husband came back and says Terry Duff long time no see and it was Tam who for a while was my next door neighbour in Alderman Road. Tam was telling me that he was hoping to get voluntary redundancy from the whisky bond in Drumchapel. On the Wednesday night we were watching the Rangers European game when he got a message through with a letter from another employee telling them they had been successful and how much they would get. The name on the letter was Margaret Bennett and I said cannot be the same one I knew 50 years ago. Tam phoned and handed me the handset, Margaret appeared and promptly shouted I know who that is, it is Terry Duff and we had a chat about families and who was still here and who wasn't. I will try and catch up with Margaret soon as our mums and dads were very good friends over the years.

My last coincidence is the strangest one yet. My father had a receding hairline and Robert, Alex and John were named after his brothers, those three had receding and then bald heads. Adam (Kenny), James and I were named after our mothers brothers and all had full heads of hair, no logic no rhyme or reason but a strange one indeed.

TERRY DUFF (WEE GLASGOW GUY)

Andy with clothes, me and Marie, Sadie, Sus, Alana, Gary, Mum, Jean, Dan, Natalie and Barry James and Caroline the stage jumpers

Bud, Jim and I circa 1978, then 2018, Kenny, James, Me and John proving hair theory

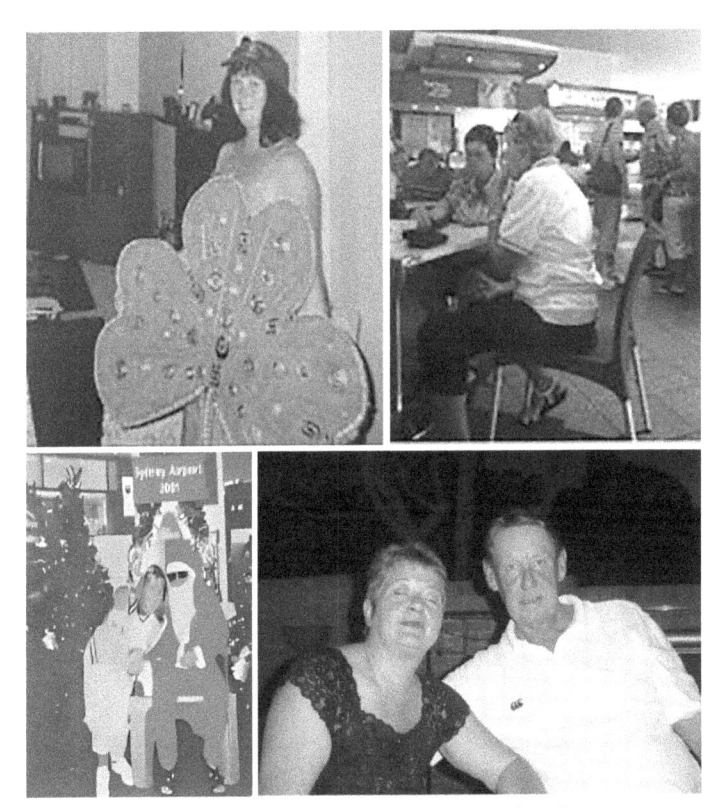

That bloody shamrock, saucy lady, Cheryl and Santa dad, our ex friend Helen and big guy Tony

TERRY DUFF (WEE GLASGOW GUY)

Boyd's 25th Anniversary, Sus, Me, Lawrence, Margaret, $606 painting and the Olympic Torch bearer

MEET YRRET FFUD

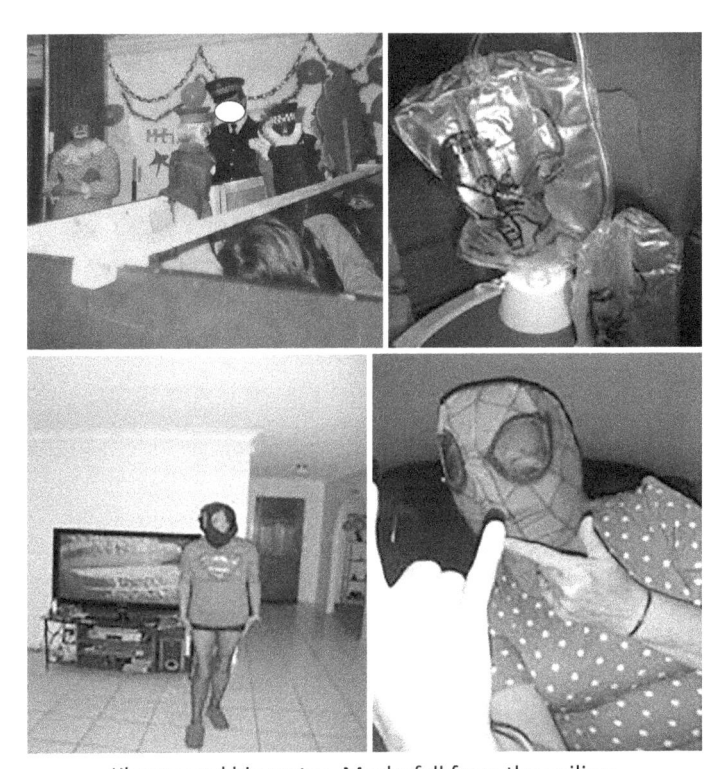

Kleeno and his mates, Masks fall from the ceiling,
Spider mum, Spider daughter

TERRY DUFF (WEE GLASGOW GUY)

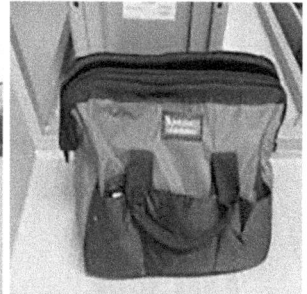

Cheryl, Mirren, Sus, Me, Mason, Mum at Eddie and Heather
wedding, Mum, Celtic legend Willie Wallace,
Sus and Eddie, Cheryl 21st Me and John and the Bunnings
bag in Yoker Bowling Club

View to Centrepoint Tower my first job, Dan and twin Babs,
Sus, Me, Eddie, Mum, Gary, David, Natalie, Sadie, Me,
Barry, Ross, Millie, Paisley and Alana last
night in Oz and the flight home

About the Author

I am a humble little Glaswegian guy who has gone through life smiling and laughing, a truly wonderful medicine. I have had my share of life's ups and down's but scraped through and still going aged 65. I always wanted to write a book and have worked on this one for many years, more to follow, who knows.